A MULTIFAMILY REAL ESTATE INVESTMENT FABLE
BUILDING WEALTH THROUGH REAL ESTATE

A LEAP OF FAITH

Discover the Secrets of Apartment Investing: Generate Wealth and Passive Income *Effortlessly*

JACOB & ARLEEN GARZA

REEP|EQUITY

100% of the proceeds from "Leap of Faith" will be donated to THRU Project

THRU Project bridges the gap between foster care and adulthood for youth who age out of the foster care system.

Exiting foster care alone at age 18 can be overwhelming. Statistics show increased rates of homelessness, unplanned pregnancy, and incarceration amongst foster alumni.

THRU Project provides youth with a history of foster care, ages 14 to 25, with a caring mentor, rent-free housing, mental health support, life skills workshops, bus passes, and cell phones.

Learn more about THRU Project at https://www.thruproject.org/

Time, not money,
is the most precious
resource we have.

Table of Contents

Foreword
by Coach Trevor McGregor

As a Real Estate Investor and High-Performance Business Coach, I've had the honor of conducting over 45,000 one-on-one coaching sessions with an incredible range of professionals, including entrepreneurs, business owners, real estate investors, doctors, attorneys, and other accomplished leaders. This extensive experience has fueled my deepest passion—helping individuals harness their full potential, dismantle obstacles, and reach extraordinary heights of success, wealth, and freedom.

What inspires me most is the privilege of working with exceptional clients across the globe. These high-achieving individuals are not only dedicated to their personal growth but also committed to uplifting others, creating a ripple effect of success and empowerment. It's truly been a rewarding journey to support and guide such visionary leaders as they transform their lives—and the lives of those around them.

A few years ago, I had the privilege of meeting Jacob Garza and his remarkable wife, Arlene Garza, from REEP Equity, and from the moment I began working with them, I could tell there was something extraordinary about them and their approach to building a phenomenal Real Estate Investment firm with their own in-house management company. Out of all the real estate principals I'd ever worked with, I had never seen such a powerful, dynamic, and heart-centered couple as Jacob and Arlene. They had an incredible passion for what they did and a track record that was outstanding as well. As they continued to grow their empire in leaps and bounds, I was fortunate enough to have a front-row seat to watch them become one of the most successful multifamily real estate firms in North America.

This book, *A Leap of Faith*, is not just another book about real estate or wealth-building. It is a rare gem that reveals a proven pathway to creating sustainable, generational wealth through one of the most powerful vehicles available today: Multifamily Real Estate Investing. Jacob and Arlene's journey has been nothing short of extraordinary; not only have they transformed their own lives, but they've also transformed the lives of their team members, their residents, and especially the lives of the thousands of investors who've partnered with them. Their story is one of resilience, vision, unwavering perseverance, and, most importantly, how hard work, smart decision-making, and a profound mindset shift can lead to true financial abundance.

In *A Leap of Faith*, Jacob and Arlene invite you into their world of multifamily investing, guiding you step by step through the nuances of this incredible investment model. Through a mix of heartwarming storytelling, insightful reflections, and actionable advice, they share the core principles that have helped them build a thriving real estate business and attract a loyal, growing community of investors. What sets this book apart even more is that Jacob and Arlene don't just show you how they do it; they reveal the deeper *why* behind their approach. In just a few short chapters, you'll discover the incredible impact their work has had, not only on their own financial success but on the lives of the families, communities, and investors they've touched along the way.

What I also love about *A Leap of Faith* is how Jacob and Arlene break down the process of investing in multifamily real estate in simple, digestible terms. They walk you through their strategies for identifying high-potential properties and then show you how they optimize and maximize their performance. You'll learn how they've leveraged their expertise to create incredible returns for their investors, and you'll also realize that you don't need to be a real estate expert or manage properties yourself to reap the rewards of this powerful asset class. This book invites you to think beyond traditional investments, embrace the power of passive income, and understand that financial freedom is not just a distant dream; it is a very achievable reality.

Perhaps most importantly, *A Leap of Faith* invites you to join an incredible community. Jacob and Arlene have built much more than a successful business; they've created a thriving network of like-minded individuals who are all working toward the same goal: financial independence and a life of purpose. Their work with REEP isn't just about making money; it's about creating a lasting, positive impact on the lives of their team, the families they serve, and the investors who partner with them.

As you read the following pages and reflect, I highly encourage you to take action. The Garzas' success story proves that multi-family real estate investing can change your life and your family's future forever.

Let their story inspire you, their wisdom guide you, and their passion ignite within you the belief that you, too, can achieve extraordinary financial abundance and live the life of your dreams.

Enjoy the journey ahead.

Sincerely,

Trevor McGregor,
Master Platinum High-Performance Business Coach and Mentor

An Invitation

My most vivid memories of my childhood are from the age of ten—Mom and Dad talking in the kitchen while she was preparing his breakfast before he left to go to work. The usual topic of their conversation was either us kids or the family's finances. I remember them talking about the fact that winter was coming—a time when the jobs typically either slowed down or stopped, and my dad would not have an income for a few months. The feeling in the pit of my stomach at hearing, "How are we going to make it?" stayed with me for years.

My name is Arleen Garza. My husband, Jacob, and I founded and run a company called REEP Equity. We invite you to learn more about us and how investing in real estate has secured our retirement. We sleep at night, as do the thousands of other families who invest alongside Jacob and me.

My mom and dad started out picking cotton in the fields of New Mexico. That was their first job as a young married couple. Eventually, my dad said, "This won't sustain our family," and they moved to Texas, where he taught himself how to read blueprints so that he could work in the oilfield construction industry. He worked his way up to a supervisor position but unfortunately passed away at the young age of forty-eight.

Fortunately, my mom was excellent at saving. How she managed to keep everything together for ten kids on $25,000 a year, I don't know. I remember overhearing the same conversation every winter: "How are we going to make it through this time of hardship?" Those savings would always be depleted after a winter with no income, and then she'd have to start over. I remember thinking, *I don't want that. There's got to be a different way to live.*

Initially, when I reached adulthood, I thought accounting was the way to go. So, I started as an accounting major. I switched to finance, however, when I realized that while there's no magic formula for security, there *is* a way to approach growing your money and managing your finances to avoid being in that position.

That realization laid the foundation for me to continue finding new ways to invest. In the banking world, we talked to our clients about traditional stocks and bonds and certificates of deposit. But after I left that corporate world, I began to really expand my awareness and understanding of alternative investments. Jacob and I founded REEP (Real Estate Equity Partners) and discovered a way to invest and craft something that benefits our investors, our tenants, and ourselves.

At REEP Equity, we locate underperforming apartment complexes, buy them, and upgrade them in order to transform them into outstanding, beautiful, safe places to live. In so doing, we create outstanding returns for our investors, who often return to invest with us again on project after project.

* * *

Hello, I'm Jacob, and Arleen's journey was a little different from mine. When I was growing up in a middle-class family of five, my father had a steady job as a union worker in a manufacturing plant, but we still lived mostly paycheck to paycheck. My mom was able to work in the home, so my family did well, but we weren't *truly* secure.

As an adult, I was a serial entrepreneur who built and sold several software companies, including one that developed property management software for property management companies. After I sold the company and made my exit, I didn't go back to the topsy-turvy and risky technology industry because I saw that it wasn't something on which I could build family legacy wealth. At that time, I turned to Arleen and said, "Arleen, I'm done with technology. Let's buy an apartment community."

My vision of REEP was always for it to be a sustainable legacy wealth business that we could grow by filling two critical needs: providing the best place for residents to live and a place for investors to passively grow their money.

For us, it was about educating ourselves… and then educating others. Most people aren't taught how to manage and grow their finances, and that's a problem. Kids today don't learn about money in school. After graduation, they rack up debt, or they don't invest, and spend what they make.

We at REEP spend a lot of time writing blogs and white papers, creating videos, holding live Q&A webinars, and reaching the public in any way we can so that people can understand how to grow, how compounding works, and how money can grow through appreciation. We locate underperforming apartment complexes and buy and upgrade them, creating those welcoming and safe places for our tenants to live that Arleen spoke about. In so doing, we create outstanding returns for our investors, who often return to invest with us again on project after project.

Impact Investing is what makes REEP stand out from other real estate investment enterprises. We're concerned with making the world better—not just for our investors but also for our employees and for the tenants who live in the communities we create. We seek to create wins for everyone with whom we are associated. That's why so many individuals, couples, and families entrust us with their investment dollars. Our hope is that after you've read the story that follows and you see how kindness, public-spiritedness, and the profit motive can dovetail, you'll want to join us.

* * *

Let's get to know each other. After reading these first few pages, you know a bit about us. This is who we are, and this is where we come from. We understand you because—like most of you—we didn't start from the heights. We came from humble backgrounds, and we appreciate the value of hard work.

If you've reached a point where *your* hard work has created the financial means for you to invest in your long-term future, and you're ready for your money to work smart on your behalf, then perhaps we should talk. If you are a Family Office and would like to know more about an investment firm that has a proven track record, we should talk.

Everyone wants to succeed . . . and yet, at the same time, most people want to live meaningful lives that bring about the best outcomes for those they love and those they serve. There are many ways to combine material and spiritual success in business. The vehicle we are privileged to provide to our investors, team members, and tenants is the world of real estate.

We hope you enjoy the story that follows and that it answers any questions and resolves any doubts you may have about investing in multifamily real estate. When you've finished reading, we look forward to hearing from you and getting to know *you* as well as you know us.

Chapter 1

It's Not a Date

Is it weird to have a crush on your dentist?

Gabriel Gerard asked himself this question as he entered the suite of offices belonging to Elena Madsen, DDS, the woman who had been his dentist for the past five years.

Not if you actually know Elena, Gabriel reminded himself. As he entered the reception area, he was immediately hit with the aroma of the soft chocolate chip cookies that were always heating up in a small oven. They were a sweet reward for having done the right thing by showing up for a cleaning or a filling.

Smart business, Gabriel thought appreciatively, as he always did when he smelled those cookies. It wasn't so crazy to have a crush on Elena Madsen, he decided. She was the whole package: not only was she smart, kind, funny, attractive and good at business, but she had strong personal values. Indeed, Gabriel's hygienist, Elizabeth (whom Elena called a "hy-genius" to add a sense of fun to the role), once told him that Elena had actually put herself through medical school as a model. She'd gone into dentistry because she wanted to do something more meaningful with her life. . . but that didn't mean that at age thirty-five, Elena didn't still turn heads.

Gabriel approached the reception desk, where he was greeted by Elena's receptionist, Jimmy, a man in his forties who had been at the dental practice for as long as Gabriel could remember.

"Gabriel!" Jimmy exclaimed with a warm smile. "You're here for a cleaning, right? We'll take you back in a moment."

Gabriel, a serial entrepreneur who admired well-run businesses, always enjoyed the brisk efficiency with which Elena ran her dental practice. He could not remember waiting more than a few minutes past his appointment. Unlike other dentists he had seen, Elena gave her "hy-geniuses" (Gabriel had to laugh every time he thought of the word) a full hour to complete a dental cleaning instead of the more customary thirty minutes. This allowed for a more relaxed experience and gave the hygienist time to educate patients and share her observations with Elena, who typically dropped in about forty minutes into the visit.

Gabriel had noticed something that other dentists tended to do: they would invalidate the hygienist's advice, saying that the work the hygienist suggested was unnecessary and that all they needed to do was "put a watch on it."

Having started and sold three successful tech companies, Gabriel knew a thing or two about sales, and he recognized the fear of rejection when he saw it. He knew that dentists were often so afraid of hearing no from a patient when they were proposing a case—especially if it was potentially painful or expensive work—that they wouldn't even ask the patient if they wanted the treatment. They would just proceed from the assumption that the treatment was unnecessary out of fear that the patient would rebel and go find another dentist. It was a lose-lose-lose situation: the hygienist felt invalidated, the patient didn't get the needed care, and the dentist lost the business.

But that wasn't how things worked in Elena's office, where nothing less than a 100 percent healthy mouth would do. Elena would never let that happen, Gabriel realized, as he idly watched an in-house video of Elena demonstrating flossing technique to a twelve-year-old boy—who, truth be told, looked just as smitten as Gabriel sometimes felt.

Instead, Elena fearlessly supported the recommendations of her "hy-geniuses," who were more highly trained and experienced than any other hygienists Gabriel had encountered in his life. They knew what to look for, and they knew how to demonstrate the need for a filling or a crown on the ginormous video screen mounted on the wall next to the dental chair. Elena had no fear of rejection whatsoever, as far as Gabriel could tell. If the patient didn't want the work, he or she would have to say so; Elena wasn't going to say it for them.

As a result, Elena's practice was thriving, and new patients often had to wait several months for an appointment. She worked six days a week in the office and often spent the fifth day in a clinic in a low-income neighborhood twenty minutes from her office, providing free care to patients who would not otherwise afford it.

When you put it all together—the efficiently run office, the high standard of care, the absolute dedication to professionalism, and Elena's charitable work—Gabriel realized he actually *looked forward* to coming to the dentist. *Who does that?* he thought.

"We'll take you back now, Gabriel" a voice said, interrupting Gabriel's reverie. It was Billie, the care coordinator, who also worked with patients to finance more expensive dental procedures when they were necessary.

"Bringing Gabriel back to Elizabeth," Billie said into her headset as if they were arranging a moon landing rather than a dental cleaning. She escorted Gabriel to the room where his hygenius worked.

Elizabeth greeted him warmly, seated him in the chair, gave him a pair of dark glasses, and began a temple massage—a custom Elena had instituted in the belief that relaxed patients were typically more receptive to care.

Gabriel inquired about Elizabeth's three children, ranging in age from twelve to seventeen. They were all doing great, she said.

Elizabeth had been the first to go to college in her family, and she prioritized education for her children. On his previous visit, she'd chided Gabriel for his failure to floss adequately, and truth be told, he'd been somewhat anxious about submitting to today's inspection. Much to his relief, she noted an improvement since last time and praised him for it.

An hour later, when Elizabeth's work was done, Elena strolled in. *Even in her office whites, she looked stylish and elegant*, Gabriel thought. He gave her a warm smile, and they shook hands.

"Elizabeth says you're flossing better," Elena said, smiling.

"I cannot bear her disapproval," Gabriel said, and all three of them laughed.

"Let's see what's going on in there," Elena said, and she gently probed Gabriel's mouth with a mirror and a small, unpleasantly sharp tool.

"Looks great," she said admiringly. "You won't be needing me for a while."

"That's disappointing to hear," Gabriel said in a slightly flirty way.

Elena could feel the heat of a blush rush into her cheeks.

"Looks like business is booming," Gabriel said, embarrassed at his breach of decorum.

"Thank you, God," Elena said, nodding happily. "I guess we're just lucky that way."

"Luck has nothing to do with it," Gabriel said firmly. "You run a great practice. It's that simple."

"Coming from you, mister serial entrepreneur," Elena said, beaming at the compliment, "that's high praise."

"I shouldn't waste any more of your time," Gabriel said, slightly embarrassed to catch himself flirting with his dentist. *I mean, who does that?* he asked himself.

"You're not wasting my time at all," Elena said. "In fact, I've been wanting to ask you something."

"Really?" Gabriel said, surprised. "Like what?"

"Well, I know you're a successful entrepreneur, so I figured you know a lot about investing," she said. "I'm thinking about getting into real estate."

Surprised by the shift in topic, Gabriel nodded.

"Great move," he said. "That's where something like 70 to 80 percent of the world's fortunes have been made. You do it right, and you can't go wrong."

Elena ran a hand through her hair.

"That's what I'm concerned about," she said. "Doing it right. I'm thinking about buying some single-family homes. I see people doing this on TV all the time. They buy them, improve them, and either flip them or rent them out. Do you know anything about that?"

"I don't know much about single-family houses," Gabriel said, looking thoughtful. "I just know I wouldn't touch them with a ten-foot pole."

"Why not?" Elena asked, looking surprised.

"Tenants and toilets," Gabriel said. "If they don't pay their rent, you can be stuck. Lawyers are expensive. If a place is vacant for a while, you've got no money coming in and plenty going out. If a toilet gets clogged at two in the morning, *you're* going to get a phone call. It just seems like a really difficult way to make money.

"In addition," he continued, "you're dependent on the rent payments to cover the mortgage and expenses. When the tenant moves out, you are without that income until you replace that tenant, and you are on the hook for those expenses."

Sitting on the edge of the stool opposite Gabriel's chair, Elena nodded.

"Yeah," she sighed. "I hear about those things. But I just thought they had to be exaggerations. I mean, it looks so easy on TV."

"Dentistry probably looks easy on TV," Gabriel countered. "But I wouldn't try to do my own dental work based on something I saw on Netflix."

"I'm just scared about the market," Elena said. "It feels like it's just sort of going nowhere right now. And it drops 30 percent once or twice a decade—and after that, it can take forever for it to just come back to even. You know what I mean?"

Gabriel nodded. "It's risky," he agreed. "I mean, over time, it always goes up, but it just seems like today there is more uncertainty than ever."

"That's why I was thinking real estate," Elena said. "You put the money in the bank, and inflation eats up whatever interest you make. And bonds are pretty safe, but there's no real upside. So that's why I was thinking single-family homes."

"I'll tell you what I'd do," Gabriel said.

"What's that?" Elena asked, staring intently at him with her piercing, cornflower-blue eyes. Gabriel got lost in those eyes for a moment but quickly snapped himself back to reality. His crush on her was a distraction that he would have to ignore somehow if he were going to have an intelligent conversation with her.

"Apartment buildings," he said.

"Apartment buildings?" Elena repeated. "I couldn't afford an apartment building! I mean, I've got enough cash to make down payments on some single-family homes. But an apartment building? That's got to cost a fortune!"

"I don't own any apartment buildings," Gabriel said, smiling. "I invest with a couple that buys apartment buildings, fixes them up, manages them, and sells them when the time comes. They're great people."

"Really?" Elena said, looking pensive. "Who are they?"

"Jacob and Arleen Garza," Gabriel said.

"Never heard of them," Elena said.

"They don't advertise," Gabriel said. "It's all word of mouth. But they're the real deal."

Elena glanced at her watch and frowned. "I've got to do a bridge right now," she said. "Buy me a cup of coffee after work today? Tell me more about the Garzas?"

Gabriel must have looked shocked because Elena quickly backtracked.

"I'm not asking you out on a date," she said. "Strictly business."

"Strictly business," Gabriel agreed. "Sure. There's a coffee shop across the street from your office. Meet you there at 5:30?"

"Perfect," Elena said. And with that, she gave Gabriel a warm smile and headed out of the hygienist's exam room.

"A date with the boss lady!" Elizabeth teased happily.

Gabriel reddened. "It's not a date," he said. "We're talking real estate."

"Sounds like a date to me," Elizabeth said, smiling, handing him a bag with a new toothbrush, floss, and mouthwash. "Use the mouthwash before your date," she said.

Gabriel rolled his eyes. "Whatever," he said, grinning, as Elizabeth led him back to the receptionist area to pay for his visit.

"And even if it were a date," Gabriel thought to himself as he gave his credit card to the receptionist, "where's the harm in that?"

Chapter 2

Coffee and an Invitation

At 5:30 on the dot, Elena strolled into the coffee shop where Gabriel was waiting for her. Gabriel marveled at her. She was beautiful. She looked like she had spent the day at the beach, not drilling and filling.

"What can I have them start for you?" he asked as she walked up to his table. "Coffee, cappuccino?"

"I don't do caffeine very much," Elena said, returning his smile. "I have so much nervous energy that I make coffee nervous! Also, coffee stains teeth. It won't be good for business if I see patients with stained teeth."

"I'm sure your patients would overlook that one flaw," Gabriel said, a bit more flirtatiously than he'd meant to.

She chuckled. "A room-temperature bottle of sparkling water would be fine."

Gabriel went to the counter to get a couple bottles of sparkling water. He was not antisocial, but he actually couldn't remember the last time he'd been on a date. *All work and no play*, he thought. *I think I'm turning into a dull boy. Not good.*

Anyway, this isn't a date, he mused to himself. *We're just here to talk about real estate. But I guess it's good practice if I ever get out there again.*

"Getting out there again" was something that had been on his mind for a long time now. Gabriel had lost his wife nearly seven years before, and the hole left in his heart by her passing had never been filled. The twin demands of his career and single fatherhood had kept him from dating—maybe for too long, he now thought.

He returned to the table. "Sparkling water for two," he said as he handed her the bottle. He noted, with gratitude, that the coffee shop was fairly empty. Just a few college students with laptops open and a couple of people reading—one a newspaper, one a book. *It's nice to have a quiet place to talk*, he thought, *even if this isn't a date.*

"So, tell me more about these mysterious Garzas," Elena said.

"Well," Gabriel began, "their way of thinking is that you're either a passive or active investor when it comes to real estate. If you're active, it means you have to manage the property. You have all the responsibilities for routine maintenance, collecting rent, unclogging toilets, painting, fixing anything that arises with the property, or hiring people to do it for you. If somebody slips and falls, you could get sued. If somebody *doesn't* slip and fall, they can still sue you.

"And sometimes it can take longer than you'd think to get a good tenant. And when you have a bad tenant, well, the eviction process is lengthy, and you could be tied up with them for a year before you see another dollar of rent from them or from anybody else. These days, eviction laws really favor the tenant—and the tenants know it—so a lot of people take advantage."

"I thought you said you didn't know anything about single-family homes," Elena said, looking confused. "How do you know so much?" she asked, surprised.

"I know a little bit," Gabriel admitted. "I just don't know how to make real money with them. The truth is, I owned six of them previously. Four of them went great, one broke even, and on the sixth one, I lost nearly as much money as I made on the four good ones. That's why I got out of the business.

"Never mind the risk, though," he continued. "The other problem was I found that I was just too busy. I run tech companies, *and* I'm a single dad. I don't exactly have time to call plumbers and deal with daily issues concerning maintenance and tenants. The whole thing seemed like a good idea at the time, and I guess, if I had stayed with it, I could have made decent money, but it was just too much effort for the reward."

Elena nodded thoughtfully. "I'm sitting on a bunch of cash," she said. "I didn't want to say that in front of Elizabeth, but I am. The practice is incredibly successful—I had a really good coach, and he showed me how to make things work great for the team, for the patients, and for the bottom line. I love being chairside, and I hate doing anything else. So now I'm chairside 85 percent of the time I'm working. It's like a dream."

"Congratulations!" Gabriel responded. "That's very impressive!"

"Thank you," Elena replied. "I hope I didn't sound like I was bragging."

"Not at all," Gabriel said. "I admire successful business owners, and that's what you are. It's exciting!

"It would be more exciting if I knew what to do with the cash," she said. "I'm actually losing money because inflation is so high. Everything I pay for, whether it's dental equipment or groceries, seems like it's gone up a lot more than that. I've got cash just sitting in a money market fund. That's not exactly how you get rich, which is why I was thinking about real estate."

"I've done five deals with the Garzas," Gabriel said. "It's simple. It's a passive investment, so I don't have to do anything. Besides, I just like them. They're nice people."

"If they're so good, why don't they advertise?" Elena asked. "After you mentioned them earlier, I looked them up online and found their website, but I really had to do some digging to learn anything about them."

"They've been doing this long enough that they don't need to advertise," Gabriel said. "I don't think they ever did, although I'm not sure. It's all just word of mouth. One happy investor tells a friend . . . or their dentist."

"So why is investing in an apartment building such a good idea? I mean, all you're getting is a piece of the rent, right?

Gabriel shook his head.

"It's much more than that," he said. "You're getting tax benefits like you can't imagine. For every $100,000 I've put into an investment with REEP—that's their company—I was able to claim something like 40,000 to $45,000 in tax write-offs the first year. And then on top of that, I'm getting mailbox money every quarter. It continues to go up because they spruce up the apartments, and then they can raise the rents.

"And then on top of that, when they sell, typically three to five years after the investment starts, they pay back almost double. The apartment complexes are worth so much more because of the renovations and the appreciated value."

"And no tenants and toilets to worry about," Elena said. "I'm intrigued."

"I'd be happy to introduce you if you wanted," Gabriel said.

"You really trust them? I mean, we're talking about real money here."

"They've never let me down," Gabriel said. "Or anybody else, as far as I know. These days, if people are less than honest, it's all over the Internet. Nobody can hide from a bad reputation anymore. But you'll never find anything negative online about the Garzas because they do things the right way."

Elena sighed. "I guess owning a bunch of houses sounds better in theory than in reality. It's a weird problem to have or to think of as a problem—having a ton of cash and nowhere to put it."

Gabriel nodded. "It's not necessarily a problem that everybody can relate to," he said. "But when it's your cash, *it is* a problem!"

"Well, I guess you would know," Elena said. "Given your own talent for making money."

Gabriel flushed. "I've had a little bit of success along the way," he admitted as modestly as he could.

"I would call getting to three exits in twelve years more than *a little* success," Elena said, teasing him.

"You looked me up," he said, at once flattered and disconcerted.

"I did. I've been asking a few of my more successful patients about what they do with their money. Most of them just want to turn me on to their money manager. They say they've 'got a guy.' But when I ask them how well their 'guy' is doing for them, they just kind of shrug. Did you know that 95% of financial advisors don't get as good a return for their client's money as the S&P 500? So, really, how good can their 'guy' really be? You're the first person who's given me an answer other than, 'Stick the money with a money manager and hope that he doesn't lose too much.'"

Gabriel laughed.

"I've got some money with a wealth manager," he said. "And you're right. I'm just happy if he doesn't lose very much. It's more about capital preservation than anything else, and just hoping you'll be there if the market does finally start going up again. But hope isn't exactly a strategy for making money."

"I'd say not," Elena said. "I don't mean to take so much of your time. I know you're a busy guy, but if you could connect me to the Garzas, that would be great."

Gabriel suddenly remembered an e-mail he'd gotten from the Garzas a week earlier. "They're actually doing a dinner for their investors next week," he said. They do this thing where investors can bring their friends, meet the Garzas, hear a little about what they do, and ask questions. I wasn't going to go, but if you'd like, I would be happy to take you and introduce you to them."

"Not if it would inconvenience you," Elena said quickly.

It would hardly be an inconvenience, Gabriel thought.

"We could go," he said noncommittally, trying not to sound as eager as he felt. Why had he never asked Elena out in the three years he'd been coming to her dental practice, he wondered to himself.

"When is it exactly?" Elena asked, opening her phone to her calendar app.

"Let me check," Gabriel said, pulling out his phone and thumbing through his e-mail. "It's this Friday. At the Palace Hotel, downtown."

"I could do that," Elena said enthusiastically.

"Umm . . . do you want to meet there?" Gabriel asked, slightly flustered at the idea of spending an evening with his very talented dentist, even if it was just to hear a pitch about real estate investing.

Elena pursed her lips anxiously. "I'm a little bit nervous about being surrounded by unfamiliar faces in unfamiliar places all by myself," she said. "I'm more comfortable if I'm with someone who can introduce me to people. What if you came by my house and picked me up?"

Gabriel could hardly believe this was happening. *It's not a date*, he reminded himself in an effort to calm the sudden quickening of his pulse. "I'd like that!" he said.

"Thanks for the advice, the sparkling water, and your time," Elena said, looking delighted to have flummoxed him. "I'll see you in front of my house on Friday at seven. How's that?"

"Perfect," Gabriel said in a voice one octave higher than his usual voice. "See you then!" he added, overcompensating by speaking in an unnaturally low tone.

Elena gave him a warm smile, picked up her bottle of water, and strolled out of the coffee shop.

<h1 style="text-align:center">Chapter 3</h1>

<h1 style="text-align:center">Dinner and an Education</h1>

"Now, you behave yourself tonight, Tony, and do everything Jill tells you to do, okay?"

Gabriel tousled his eight-year-old son's dark brown hair and chuckled. Tony irritably waved his father's hand away. "Yeah, Dad, I know. I'm not a baby."

"Don't worry about us, Gabe," said Jill. She patted Tony's shoulder affectionately. "We'll have a good time, so you make sure to do the same. I don't think I've seen you go out on a date the whole time I've known you!"

Inwardly, Gabriel winced. He'd been a widower for the six years Jill had known him. Tony's mom, Judith, had passed away a few months before they met after losing a brief struggle with breast cancer. Judith had never been conscientious about medical checkups and screenings, and the disease had gone undetected until it was too late: by the time the doctors discovered what was wrong with her, it had reached stage 4. A few months later, pressured by the urgent need to return to work and earn a living, Gabriel had searched desperately for a reliable, trustworthy babysitter. A neighbor had recommended Jill, and she had been his go-to sitter ever since.

"It's *not* a date," Gabriel replied, a bit more sharply than he'd intended. He quickly softened his tone. "I'm just helping her to make some investment decisions. Besides, she is my dentist. She's probably not even *allowed* to date her patients."

Jill smiled wryly. "Whatever you say," she said, clearly not believing him.

"Well, you two have fun while I'm gone," Gabriel said a bit awkwardly, and he walked out the door.

Getting into his red 1996 Porsche Boxster, he mused on what Jill had said. She'd only been teasing him, but the remark had gotten under his skin a little bit. The truth was, he *hadn't* dated anyone in the six years since Judith's passing—and that was probably why Jill was so keen to imagine that he was out on a date. For the first two or three years after becoming a widower, grief had kept him from even considering reentry into the dating pool, and work had provided him with an excellent excuse not to.

But as time passed and his grief subsided, Gabriel had begun to realize that work was no excuse to withdraw from life . . . and that it was beginning to interfere with his duties as a father. One night, he'd come home late—it must have been nearly ten o'clock —to find Jill buzzing with excitement. Tony, for the very first time, had tied his own shoes with no assistance. It was a huge milestone in the life of any parent . . . and he'd missed it. The kid was in bed by that time, oblivious to the excitement he'd caused, and Gabriel felt guilty that a babysitter rather than a parent had witnessed this big event.

He decided that a career change was in order. He'd done well for himself as a software engineer and even better as a tech entrepreneur, but now he wanted—no, *needed*—some way to make a passive income so he could be 100 percent present in his son's life. Lacking a mother, the boy now needed Gabriel to be twice the father he had been up to that point.

Gabriel's friend Don had suggested real estate investment as the solution to his problem and had brought him to one of the Garzas' investor dinners—just Gabriel himself was bringing Elena tonight—and the rest, as the cliché goes, was history. Gabriel still had modest investments in a number of tech companies, but the passive income provided by the Garzas' apartment syndications meant he no longer needed to devote his time to running a business in order to maintain the lifestyle that he and Tony enjoyed.

"In one hundred feet, turn right," his phone said, breaking his train of thought. Elena had given him a North Central address in Deerfield, which meant she was doing all right for herself. This evening's outing wasn't a date, but Gabriel had to admit to himself that he had a rapidly growing list of justifications for his crush on the comely dentist.

"Your destination is on the left," said his phone. Gabriel parked his Porsche in front of Elena's house, thinking, *If this isn't a date, then why does my stomach feel so weird?* He hadn't felt this nervous since before he'd gotten married.

He killed the engine and got out of the car, but before he could take two steps toward the house, Elena was already out the door, walking briskly toward him. "Ooh, not just a Porsche, but a *red* one! If you're trying to impress me, it's working!"

"Hah! If this were a date, I guess I would be!" he said, holding the passenger door open for her. For a tech entrepreneur, he was very much in the habit of behaving like an old-fashioned gentleman.

"Which it's not," Elena replied, gracefully seating herself as he shut the door behind her. Her tone was suddenly much less flirtatious, as though she'd caught herself behaving inappropriately. As he got back into the driver's seat, Gabriel felt a tiny pang of disappointment, which he assuaged by starting the car and gunning the engine. The Porsche took off like a rocket. Elena screamed at the sudden acceleration and laughed with delight. "Attaboy!" she said.

Gabriel chuckled, affecting a James Bond-esque nonchalance and hoping he was pulling it off. "Well, what's the point of owning one of these big-kid toys if you're not going to drive it like it's meant to be driven?"

"A man after my own heart!" Elena replied. And then there was a beat of awkward silence.

"So, where is this dinner?" she asked after a few seconds.

"At the Palace Hotel downtown," he replied. "Probably about twelve miles from here. I'll have us there in maybe ten minutes."

Why would you say that his left brain whispered to him *unless this is a date and you're trying to impress her?*

* * *

Almost exactly ten minutes later, they arrived at the Palace Hotel. Gabriel handed his keys to the valet and offered Elena his arm so he could escort her properly. Date or no date, it seemed like the classy thing to do.

The concierge directed them to the dining room, where a well-dressed hostess escorted them to a small table where two other guests, a young woman and an older man, were already seated. "Hi there!" the woman said. "My name's Cara, and this is my father, Dan."

"A pleasure," Gabriel said. "I'm Gabriel, and this is my friend Elena. I take it you're here to learn about apartment syndications?"

Dan laughed. "No, Cara's an old hand at this by now," he said, in a thick New York accent that sounded weird and exotic to Gabriel and Elena's native Texan ears.

"But there's always more to learn," Cara said. "I've been doing apartment syndications for a few years now in Florida and Phoenix, and I'm considering investing in a building or two here in San Antonio. I like what I've heard about the Garzas so far, and I want to see whether they live up to their reputation."

"What is that reputation, exactly?" Elena said.

"Honesty, above all else," Gabriel said. "Sorry, Cara, I didn't mean to jump in so rudely."

"No worries," Cara said. "But Gabriel's right; the Garzas have a reputation not just for transparency but also for fair dealing and ethical behavior. They keep all their property management activities in-house and treat the people who work for them *very* well."

"Really? What do they—" Elena stopped speaking as the lights abruptly went down, and a soft spotlight shone on a small podium at the front of the room. A well-dressed, dark-haired man sitting at a table at the front of the room got up, took his place behind the podium, and began to speak:

"Good evening, everyone, and welcome to this year's REEP investor dinner. My name is Jacob Garza. I hope you've all taken the opportunity to socialize and get to know one another, and I'm sure you'll all enjoy the lovely dinner that the Palace Hotel's talented kitchen staff have prepared for us.

"Before we eat, however, Arleen and I would like to talk to you about why we're all here tonight. We all want the same things: We want security for the future, especially in these uncertain times. We want to work with people we know we can trust in an increasingly amoral and unethical world. We want a safe place to put our money, a place where it won't be subject to the volatility of the stock market. And then we want to be able to get on with our lives, secure in the knowledge that our investments do not require time-consuming, energy-sapping micromanagement on our part. Our most valuable possession is our free time.

"We began our career in real estate in 2012. I had sold my software company *a few years before*, and we had some money to invest; we had some goals, and like many of you, we were looking for an investment that would cash-flow and grow. We wanted to pay less in taxes, not more in taxes. We were worried about the stock market; just like now, the stock market was very volatile.

"Like many of you, we felt behind and were looking for a stable investment. I worried that trusting the stock market and relying only on my 401(k) wouldn't give me the future I wanted.

We needed to be in control of our future and what we did to grow our money.

"Our first investment was buying a twenty-four-unit apartment complex. We did everything: we were the manager, the handyman, and the rent collector. And we learned a lot. We learned the best methods and what to avoid. We learned how to invest in real estate and how to leverage that investment to grow it faster than anything else we had done.

"Over the next twelve years, we got better and better at managing investment properties and leveraging those investments to grow and create the life we wanted—then, now, and in our future.

"Thirty-five deals and over 5,800 doors later, we have hundreds of millions of dollars in assets. More importantly, we've improved the homes and communities of the people who live in our buildings.

"And we know this is the most stable, reliable, and sustainable way to invest. We believe that multifamily real estate investing is the best way to grow your investments for retirement in an uneven stock market, pay less in taxes, and improve your community and the lives of others at the same time.

"In the past fifteen years, we have helped thousands of people **just like you** grow their investments, pay less in taxes, protect against inflation, and protect their capital by including them as investors in our real estate deals.

"And so, in the next twenty minutes, I'd like to show you why multi-family real estate investment makes sense for you. We'll show you how to make money, how to pay less in taxes, and whom you should invest with and why.

"Most of you are here tonight because you've come to the conclusion that investing in real estate is the safest and most potentially lucrative thing you can do with your money. Obviously, I happen to agree."

The audience laughed politely at Jacob's joke. Gabriel chuckled, even though he'd heard it before; it was a good line, after all. Looking over at Elena, however, he noticed she was *not* laughing. Her eyes were intently focused on the figure behind the podium, her brow furrowed in concentration.

Elena, for her part, was mesmerized. Jacob was speaking aloud some of the very thoughts that had been at the forefront of her mind for months.

Jacob continued, "But all real estate investments are not alike. Many of you are no doubt still considering investing in single-family homes. 'I can buy this cheap old house,' you're thinking, 'and I can fix it up and remodel it to increase its value and then flip it. Or better yet, I can rent it and create a never-ending revenue stream!'

"Sometimes this works out . . . but often the headaches are far greater than we anticipate. And so are the risks. Unexpected repair costs are incredibly common in single-family homes. And a house that fails an inspection and has to remain unoccupied while you continue to pour money into it isn't an investment—it's a money pit.

"More than that, it's an *active* investment. If you're renting a single-family home—or any kind of rental property—you're responsible for its upkeep. You're burdened by the 'two T's'— toilets and tenants. If a toilet backs up in the middle of the night, you have to go fix it or hire someone to do it for you—which is expensive. You're also the one who has to vet those tenants before they ever move in. And if you misjudge them, or a background check fails to reveal something disqualifying, *you're* the one on the hook for that. You're the one who has to evict the tenant—which often means going to court—and you're the one paying the property taxes and other expenses until a suitable replacement tenant can be found. And that can sometimes take months . . ."

Gabriel glanced at Elena again and saw that she looked horrified. He whispered, "Are you okay?"

"Yeah," she said quietly. "I'm just thinking about how I would have managed to run a dental practice under the conditions he's describing. It's the kind of mistake that could have ruined me, and I guess I'm a little disconcerted by the thought."

"That's why I wanted you to hear his pitch first-hand," Gabriel said. "I'm not as persuasive as Jacob. He's been in this game a long time, and he knows what he's talking about."

Jacob went on, "An apartment syndication, on the other hand, is a *passive* investment. Your only commitment is financial; everything else is taken care of for you. Active investors—general partners like Arleen and me—do all the legwork, while limited partners—folks like you—simply sit back and collect the return on their investments. We find the property and inspect it, we get the loan, we handle any renovations that need to be done, and we find tenants. We also handle any issues the tenants may have, and we collect the rent. Your money goes into the building . . . and your time remains your own."

Jacob's audience applauded loudly. Elena noticed they all seemed much more engaged now than when he'd begun speaking. *He's a great speaker,* she thought. *But more important, I guess . . . what he's saying makes sense.*

"Thank you for your attention," Jacob said. "Now, I'd like to turn you over to my wife, Arleen, and we'll have a brief Q&A session. Then we can all have a good meal and get to know one another!"

Arleen rose from her seat and took her husband's place at the podium. "Thank you, Jacob," she said. "So, now that you've all heard the advantages of our value proposition expressed in broad strokes, who has a question about the nitty-gritty details?"

Having previously attended a similar presentation, Gabriel was in passive-spectator mode . . . so it startled him when Cara, seated just to his right, raised her hand. He hadn't expected his table to be the focus of the room's attention, even for a moment.

Arleen acknowledged Cara: "Yes, the young lady in the pretty red blouse. What would you like to know?"

"Hi, Arleen," she said. "My name is Cara Wright, and I'm an accredited investor with a few years of experience in apartment syndications. My question is . . . what makes you different from other firms in the syndication field? Why should we invest with you, specifically?"

"That's an excellent question," Arleen said. "And I have a two-word answer: *In-house management*. Or I guess maybe that's three words, isn't it?" The whole room laughed appreciatively; Arleen clearly had a knack for charming a crowd, and she continued.

"In general, what differentiates us is experience; it's a successful track record; it's transparency. Your investment dollars stay with REEP because we have our own management company. So, as soon as we close a property, we manage our investors' money all the way until the property sells. Everything is done in-house. Other firms use third-party management companies; after they close on a property, they hand it over to another company that brings in their team and their approach to the management of it. But for us, it's important that from day one up through closing, the vision for what we are planning to do with that property is shared. It's ingrained in our team, so the minute we take over, they hit the ground running to make the upgrades to the property, to make it a better community, to drive rents, fees, and all of the things that make a property more valuable. On a weekly basis, we monitor how well we are doing to reach the business plan for that property.

"Now, to be clear, there are some great third-party management companies doing good work in the industry. For us as owners, however, it's about knowing, day to day, what's happening at every one of our properties. And that's why we started our own management company. We have control over whom we hire, and we have control over the policies we implement to keep our team happy. Because if the team is happy, the residents are happy, knowing that a happy team is going to take care of them.

"If we didn't have in-house management, those communications might still happen ... or they might not. Because somebody else managing the property is going to be guided by somebody else's philosophy and by somebody else's approach to taking care of the team and the residents. You never take care of anything better than you care for what belongs to you.

"With our own management, we get to vet our people because those people are going to be around our tenants and their children. We conduct rigorous background checks. We're invested in making sure that we've got high-quality individuals, not just people who are good at their jobs, but *decent* people whom we can trust around a single woman in a unit if a handyman has to go in and fix something.

"We also have some proprietary tests that we give to job applicants to get an idea of how they think and what they know. We talk a lot about why our people are important to us and why their integrity matters. We've built a very special culture, and we've done it by treating our people well! We give them great benefits. We give them time off. We have a 401(k) plan. We even have a program that lends them money between pay periods when they need it for an emergency, and all these benefits are things that you really don't see in this industry.

"Finally, we really *train* our people. We're really good at professionally and personally developing all our staff so that their career trajectories with us point upward. Again, we've found that if you keep your team happy, you keep the residents happy . . . and if you keep the residents happy, they will pay the rent. They will tell their aunts and uncles and brothers-in-law about you, and that's how we build communities. That's our secret, right there."

The audience applauded, and when the applause had died down, a young, blond-haired man stood up and raised his hand. "My name is Leo Stotch," he said, "and I'm a first-time investor. My question is, exactly how do you make money with these investments?"

"Making money from multi-family investments is not difficult," Arleen said. Every month, everyone pays rent. Out of that rent, we pay expenses, and the leftover is divided up among our investors.

"At REEP, we have several built-in ways to supercharge that investment. One: we buy the right properties—ones that are underperforming for the area. We improve them and raise the rent, and we have a magic formula.

"Two: fees and amenities. I'm talking about adding pet fees, parking fees, etc., and charging extra for a washer and dryer in the unit.

"Three: the in-house decision-making I mentioned earlier enables us to cut down on execution timelines, which means investors get faster turnarounds on their money.

"So, in a nutshell, the business plan with every property we buy is to collect the rent, make renovations in order to increase the value of the property, and then sell the building at a higher price than we bought it for. So, between the rent collection and the resale, you effectively get paid twice."

Seeing yet another raised hand in the crowd, Arleen called on the hand's owner. "Yes, sir, what's your question?"

"Thank you. Earlier, you mentioned that there are tax advantages to your investment model. Could you elaborate on that, please? How do you pay less in taxes?"

"Well," Arleen said, "You should talk to your accounting professional if you want a deep dive into the specifics, but my short answer for now is that there are huge tax advantages. If you haven't invested in multifamily before, the government allows you to depreciate the investment you own. This means a portion of the property is depreciating in value, and you get to write that off on your taxes.

"And here's the beauty: you can front-load that depreciation each year, allowing you to write off a lot of your gains. This is the beauty of multi-family investing. You can't do this with single-family homes. And not only does it work in your real estate investment, but it might also cover some gains you have from other businesses you have. You can even carry over those losses from one year to the next. And if you don't use the depreciation losses, you can carry that forward to offset future income and gains. Or to offset the gain you will make when the property sells at a higher price than we bought it."

Dan spoke suddenly, without raising his hand, his deep-voiced New York accent booming in Elena's left ear, causing her to shift her position a little. "What investment criteria do you use?" he said.

Arleen began to list her criteria, ticking them off on the fingers of her left hand. "We look at job growth and income growth in the region, and we only look at properties in low-crime metro areas of two million or more, in landlord-friendly states. And we are conservative at projecting rent growth and expense growth, which is often based on our own portfolio since we own in every market we invest in."

The Q&A continued for about ten more minutes, and then, finally, dinner was served, much to Elena's relief. "That presentation was fascinating," she said, "and it's given me a lot to think about . . . but if dinner had been served five minutes later, my stomach would have jumped out of my body and eaten the rest of me!"

"Light lunch?" Gabriel asked.

"No lunch at all," Elena replied, already wolfing down her chicken parmesan. "For the third time this week."

"Hah!" said Dan. "I remember those days before I retired. That's the life of an entrepreneur. Either you've got no time to eat—"

Gabriel finished for him. "—or you're so busy you forget about eating entirely!" The two men clinked glasses.

"Elena," Dan said, "that may be the best possible illustration of the benefits of passive investment. Before I retired, my daughter used to say I'd still be working ten years after I was dead."

"And you never would have finished, would you?" said a voice behind them. It was Jacob Garza. "May I join you?" he asked.

"By all means," Gabriel said.

Jacob pulled out an empty chair, and as he sat down, he recognized Gabriel.

"Gabriel! A pleasure to see you again! I hope you're back here because you're happy?"

"I am indeed," Gabriel replied. "and I wanted to share that happiness with my friend Elena here."

"Wonderful! And I do hope you're all enjoying your meals," he said. "Perhaps more important, though, what did you think of what you heard tonight? Can I answer any questions for you?"

"I think my father and I are pretty well sold," Cara said. "I'm Cara, and he's Dan, by the way. I'll have my assistant call your office tomorrow, and we'll arrange a call."

"Excellent, Cara," Jacob said, beaming. "I look forward to it."

"I think I probably *do* have a few questions, to be honest," Elena said. "But it's been a long day, and my brain is a bit overtaxed at this point. Where can I go if I want to dig up a little more information tomorrow when I'm better rested?"

Jacob pursed his lips and thought for a moment. "Well . . . how would you like to tour one of our properties with me?"

Elena was so startled she nearly spat out the mouthful of food she was chewing. "Wow," she said. "I thought you were just going to give me a business card and direct me to your website or something."

Jacob laughed. "I might have," he said. But as it happens, I have a walk-through scheduled tomorrow."

"What do you mean 'walk-through?'"

"I visit the properties every other month," Jacob replied. "Or at least every quarter. I hop in our REEP Sprinter van and I make the rounds and just walk the properties. I do that for a few reasons: One, I want the people who live there to know who we are. I want them to know we're involved and concerned with their well-being.

"Two, because I *am* concerned with their well-being, I want to make sure everything is being run the way we want it to be run—that our high standards are being maintained. Three, I get to have face time with our REEP site employees. They are the real heroes at REEP. They are the ones who make the magic happen. They are the ones who execute the business plan. And that's probably the most rewarding part of the business: getting out there and seeing our employees and residents as real people rather than as abstract numbers on a spreadsheet."

Elena was impressed. "I'd love that," she said. "My practice is closed for the weekend, so I have time tomorrow whenever you want to get together." She fished a business card out of her purse—a simple, no-nonsense little piece of cardboard that simply read, in Ariel-font block letters, "Elena Madsen, DDS, Cosmetic and General Dentistry, (210) 555-SMIL."

Jacob took the card solemnly. "I'll call you at 9:00 AM," he said. "Gabriel, you're welcome to come along, of course. And you, too, Cara and Dan."

Cara shook her head. "I have a flight back to Phoenix tomorrow morning," she said. "And my father's headed to Houston to visit an old college buddy."

"I'll be happy to come along, though," Gabriel said.

He hoped he didn't sound as excited and eager as he felt.

Chapter 4

A Walk-Through

Elena stood outside her front door, watching the road for Gabriel's approach. They'd agreed that he would pick her up, and the two of them would go together to accompany Jacob on one of his property walk-throughs. Gabriel had texted her when he left the house about fifteen minutes before and was now due to arrive any moment. It was 9:35 AM, and Jacob was expecting them at 10:00.

She felt unaccountably nervous, and that irritated her. She had always prided herself on her ability to keep a tight rein on her emotions, and it bothered her to find herself so susceptible to Gabriel's strange combination of sad eyes and boyish charm.

The sad eyes were no big mystery, she supposed. She knew he was a widower—although his wife was now several years gone. On the other hand, maybe it was just the way his face was shaped that made his eyes look that way. It lent his face an air of tragedy and depth, which she found attractive—especially because that air was often belied by his easy sense of humor.

That good humor and his friendly, flirtatious manner were also easy to explain if one thought about it for a minute. Some might have chalked it up to a psychological defense mechanism of some kind (which was indeed a possibility), but in her experience, people who had experienced terrible sorrows often developed a new perspective on life. They could become more resilient, eager to appreciate all of life's blessings in the moment because they understood first-hand how fragile those blessings were.

As the car approached, she saw that it was also the wrong color; Gabriel's Boxster had been red, and this car was a vivid canary yellow.

The car got closer, and she could see that it *was* a Porsche—but a Cayman 981, not a Boxster. *Geez*, she thought, *is it me, or are Porsches suddenly everywhere?* She thought about an article she'd once read on the Baader-Meinhof effect—the phenomenon that causes us to see a thing everywhere once it is fixed in consciousness. *Nah*, she thought. *Just coincidence.*

But then the Cayman slowed and stopped in front of her house, and she could see that it *was* Gabriel after all.

Leaving the engine running, he stepped out of the car and walked around to open the passenger door for her. *Ever the gentleman*, she thought, before scolding herself again.

"Wow, I didn't know you had two of these!" she said.

"Hah! I've got five, actually!"

Gabriel got into the driver's seat, and if he was at all discomfited by the strange little moment they shared—or if he'd even noticed it—he gave no sign. "I buy them used and rebuild them myself," he said.

Elena was silent for a moment. "Wow, that's some hobby!" she finally said. As soon as the remark escaped her lips, she winced at the lameness of it. He made her feel like a schoolgirl, and unwittingly, he'd just inflamed the internal debate she was having.

This is **not** *a date,* she reminded herself. Again.

Maybe not, said the voice on the other side of the debate. *But still . . . what a man!*

"I find the work relaxing," Gabriel said. "And it gives me a chance to bond with Tony. He's fascinated by the loud sound of the engine, and he likes to watch me work on my cars. Plus, I think it's good for a kid to be exposed to how complicated things work, and I like showing him. It develops character traits like patience and curiosity. Besides, he's going to grow up well-to-do, so I think it's important for him to develop a healthy respect for the art of working with your hands."

With the right investments, she supposed, she could get to a place where she depended less on her practice, or having to be at the office each day and could maybe even allow it to shrink a little bit. That would leave her more time for a normal personal life . . . if that was what she wanted.

She suddenly realized that while she'd been lost in thought, Gabriel had been talking about his Porsche collection, a subject she found extremely interesting, and she hadn't been paying attention. Cursing the brain fog that seemed to have overtaken her in the past few days, she refocused her mind on their conversation and made an effort to better contribute to it.

* * *

The place where they were meeting Jacob was a garden-style apartment complex in Uptown Central, about half a mile from McAllister Park and less than a mile from San Antonio International Airport. *Too bad Cara and Dan didn't realize how close to the airport this place was located,* Elena thought. *Maybe they could have come with us after all.*

Despite its proximity to the airport, the neighborhood had an open, almost rural feel to it; trees were abundant, and tall buildings were not. Starcrest Drive was nearly an open highway, which had enabled Gabriel to again show off his willingness to give a Porsche a proper workout. (Elena, once again, had been suitably impressed.)

Gabriel turned off Starcrest Drive and entered the apartment complex's parking lot. They were a few minutes early, but they found Jacob already waiting for them there, leaning against his own car. Gabriel parked and killed the engine, and he and Elena exited the Cayman.

As they walked toward his car, Jacob called out to them, "Good morning!"

"Good morning, Jacob," Elena said. "I hope we haven't kept you waiting."

"Not at all," Jacob replied. "I just got here myself a couple of minutes ago."

They were surprised to see Arleen.

"Good morning, Gabriel and Elena. I couldn't resist tagging along since we are particularly proud of this property, the great price we bought it for, and how well it has performed."

Gabriel looked up and scanned the expansive campus. Attractively landscaped paths and small, neatly trimmed lawns separated buildings that appeared to comprise three or four apartment units apiece. "This is a pretty impressive little community, Jacob," he said.

Jacob started walking, and Elena and Gabriel followed him. "I'm glad you like it," he said. "The moment we saw it, we knew it would be a good investment."

"How did you find this place?" Elena asked.

"I find the properties," Arleen replied. "Once a property is identified through a broker, whether it is on the market or off the market, our team looks at it in person. They learn all they can about why the Seller is selling, how long they have owned the property, and how they have managed it. In the case of this place, the previous owners had owned it for eight years and took great care of the bones. However, we realized a good coat of paint, xeroscaping, and some updates on the interior would allow us to capitalize on what the Seller had not done.

"When my team goes to look at any building or apartment complex, they first check to see what might be wrong with it—for example, has maintenance been deferred? Would we and our investors find ourselves on the hook for an inordinate amount of repair work? Is there wood rot, or is the paint peeling or fading? Things like that. We repair all major items upfront, so as monthly rental income comes in, it's used for normal expenses (office salaries, make-readies, landscape, routine unit maintenance repairs), and then there's cash flow left over for investors. The key is having experience in the due diligence Arleen talked about last evening.

"Then, before an offer is finalized on a property, I will tour it personally. I am looking for any and every factor that might have a bearing on the residents' quality of life or the value of our investment. What's around that property? Is it a good neighborhood? Is it a *safe* neighborhood? Are there schools nearby, and are they schools that are rated well? Are there churches? Convenient shopping? Investments from the city?

"I also visit with the manager to learn as much as she can about the residents themselves. Where do your residents work? How would you characterize the culture of the community? Is it a lively place or a pretty quiet place at night? If there are rowdy residents, we have to take that into account. No one wants to live in a loud place where you can't sleep at night. So, that's actually kind of a trick question to hear what they say about it. Most of them will say, 'It's pretty quiet around here.'

"And while I am asking questions, I look around to get a sense of whether it's a nice-enough looking place, the curb appeal . . . and whether there's potential for us to make it look even better in the future. It is what we call 'adding value' so that residents will find the extra value for the rent they will pay."

Elena nodded thoughtfully. "I have to say, Jacob and Arleen, while I haven't yet made any kind of decision about this, I do like how hands-on you folks are."

Jacob smiled. "Thank you. As Arleen said in her speech last night, most guys like us buy properties and hand them off to a third party. Then, they mostly wash their hands of the day-to-day responsibilities of ownership. We don't do that. Isn't that right, sweetheart?"

"That's right, Jacob. That's what gives us the certainty we will have cash flow." Arleen replied.

"I'm glad," Elena said. "Getting back to the topic of the purchase of the property, once you give the green light, Arleen, how long does the remainder of the process take?"

"When we first put the property under contract to buy it, we do the appraisal, we get third party inspections, we get the loan, and we raise the money from our investors, and it's usually a sixty- to ninety-day process from the point we get it under contract." Arleen further clarified, "We've done 33 of these, and our lender considers us a preferred borrower, so that never hurts," she said with a smile.

As they walked past the first building, closest to the parking lot, they saw a woman sitting on her patio in a folding lawn chair, reading a book. At the sound of their voices, she looked up and then hurriedly put the book down, got up, and began walking toward them.

"Jacob!" she called out as she approached.

Gabriel raised an eyebrow and smiled. "The residents all know you by face and name?" he asked, incredulous.

Jacob chuckled. "No," he said. "Most of them don't. But Mrs. Adams lives right next to the parking lot and likes to spend a lot of time on her patio, so we've met quite a few times before. She's usually the first person I see when I arrive for a walk-through."

Mrs. Adams reached the group, and Jacob politely made introductions. He then turned to Mrs. Adams and said, "So what can I do for you, Abby?"

"My air conditioning is on the fritz," she said. "It's like a sauna in my apartment."

Elena felt a pang of sympathy for the woman. It was still morning, but the day was already a hot one and would probably get much worse well before noon.

"Oh my," Jacob said. "Did you call maintenance to report the problem?"

"Yes, I did. They said they'd get someone on it right away." She suddenly looked a little bit embarrassed. "So, I guess I didn't really need to buttonhole you about it. I'm sorry to bother you. I just thought you should know, I guess."

"No need to apologize, Abby. I *do* want to know about these kinds of things. We care about our residents' quality-of-life issues, and we take them very seriously. I'll double-check to make sure that something is being done."

"Thank you, Jacob," Abby said. And with that, she turned around, walked back to her chair, and returned to her book.

"This is exactly the kind of thing I'm looking for when I do these walk-throughs," Jacob said to Elena and Gabriel. "Now, don't misunderstand—I'm a businessman, not a landlord, and I generally don't have the time for these kinds of day-to-day minutiae. But even though I most likely don't have any part at all to play in solving *The Mystery of the Broken Air Conditioner*, that interaction we just had boosts Abby's confidence in the system that supports her home—and that, in turn, makes her feel happier and more comfortable living here, even when something isn't going right. So, if you'll follow me, the first thing I'm going to do is take a little walk round to the other side of her unit and take a look at that AC unit myself."

Arleen proudly commented, "Jacob loves this side of the business; taking care of the resident is always our first priority!"

As they rounded the corner, they saw that the door to the little shed that housed the AC unit was open. Inside, a uniformed maintenance man was already on his knees in front of the dysfunctional machine, tinkering with it.

"Good morning, Danny," said Jacob.

Startled, Danny jumped and let out a small yelp. Engrossed in his work, he clearly hadn't heard them coming. "Geez, Mister Garza! Where did you come from?"

"Sorry, didn't mean to sneak up on you," Jacob said. "I just happened to be passing through and thought I'd look into Mrs. Adams's air conditioning problem . . . although I see you're already hard at work on it."

"Yeah, I *think* it's a blown capacitor," Danny said. "But it's gonna take me a while to nail it down for sure."

They chatted for a few minutes, and most of what they said went right over Elena's and Gabriel's heads. Elena was as fine a dentist as the state of Texas had ever produced, but she knew approximately zilch about HVAC systems. Unable to follow their conversation, her mind idly soaked in details about Danny himself instead—and she noticed the peculiar-looking blue vest Danny was wearing over his uniform. *What on Earth is that for?* she thought. *It must be awfully hot under there.*

Jacob and Danny finished their conversation, and Danny went back to work while the three of them went back around to the front of the building.

"Excuse me a moment," Jacob said. "I'm just going to let Mrs. Adams know that her air conditioning may not be restored for a few hours." He went back to Abby's patio, and Elena and Gabriel made small talk about the heat while they waited for him to return and resume their little tour.

A minute later, Jacob returned, and they all resumed walking. Unable to contain her curiosity, Elena said, "I noticed your handyman was wearing a heavy, odd-looking vest over his uniform. It seems a little warm today for extra layers. What's that all about?"

"That's a cooling vest," Jacob replied. "And it does just what the name implies. We have a bunch of initiatives to keep our team cool in the midst of these heat waves that have been occurring in our market. That includes buying special cooling vests that have ice packs built into them, so if the maintenance team is running around fixing air conditioners or what have you, they stay nice and cool. We also have cooling stations. We have all kinds of initiatives to make sure that they stay healthy.

"And of course, we're concerned about residents, too; we've actually been sending them some tips on how they can stay healthy during high temperatures, what they can do in their units to minimize their electrical cost, and still stay cool and comfortable."

"That's nice to hear," Gabriel said. "I've known Danny for all of five minutes now, but I like him already, and I'd hate to think he was suffering, doing a tough job on a hot day like this."

"Yes, Danny's a friendly, likable guy," Jacob said. "He's a perfect example of the kind of person we like to hire. First and most obviously important, he's a first-rate HVAC mechanic. But just as important to us, he has those vital soft skills we look for. It's about things like walking into a resident's home, being respectful in what they do, putting on those little shoe covers that protect the residents' carpets and furniture, having their tools ready, saying hello to the resident if they happen to be there, leaving them the right documentation, explaining to them what they're going to do before they do it, and so forth.

"And just as I said about my encounter with Mrs. Adams a few minutes ago, my encounter with Danny this morning is exactly the kind of thing I'm seeking out when I do these walk-throughs. First thing and foremost, I want to maintain a rapport with the employees. I want to see how they're doing personally. Their well-being is very important to us, and that's why, within our industry, we're considered one of the very best firms to work for—maybe *the* best, if that doesn't sound too immodest."

They walked on, and Jacob described various amenities as they passed them. "As you can see," he said, pointing up ahead to their right, "we have a beautiful pool here, and many of the units have an excellent view of it. Cleaning and checking the chlorine and pH levels is done daily, as it should be . . . which wasn't always done under previous management, I'm afraid."

Arleen added, "Great service from our maintenance techs and great amenities help distinguish us from the competition. We look at that when we buy also so that we are able to give residents other reasons to live with us—dog parks, fitness centers, and pools are top reasons that drive potential residents to pick where they live."

* * *

Jacob and Arleen were good company, and the hour Gabriel and Elena spent with them passed quickly. On their way back to the parking lot, they came across Danny, returning from his truck with a different toolbox.

"Keep up the good work, Danny," Jacob said.

"Great to see you, Danny. Thanks for all you do," Arleen added.

"It's my job!" Danny beamed. "By the way, I want to thank you for lunch last month. I have worked at this property for nine different owners, and this is the first time anybody has treated us this well. I feel like a VIP! I had a great time, and it was one of the best meals I've ever had in my life!"

"It's our pleasure, Danny, as always."

As Danny walked back toward his battle with Mrs. Adams's air conditioning unit, Gabriel looked at him quizzically. "Do you regularly eat lunch with your maintenance people?"

Jacob laughed. "Only three times a year. And not just maintenance people. We include leasing staff, assistant managers, and managers. We also bring in our underwriters, asset managers, marketing, HR, and accounting... the entire REEP organization."

He looked over at Arleen, "We love meeting with the site teams. There are twenty- three sites, and there are a hundred or so people whom we don't get to see or interact with otherwise. So, we rent out this gigantic conference center space, and we feed them lunch. It's a nice place, and the lunch is catered. We shut down for a whole day, and we talk about the deals we are doing, underwriting, and any other concerns that any employee may have.

"We even bus people in from our Houston office—on nice buses, with TVs and snacks. I think the teams from Houston will show up at 10:00 AM. We all pile into this gigantic conference room. We open up and share success stories with them right off the bat, and then we talk about where we're going as a company, vision-wise, what's happening in the markets, et cetera. Finally, we break for lunch and enjoy some camaraderie, and at around 3:30, everyone heads home.

Elena was agog. "Let me get this straight: You bring your maintenance people to a conference, you bus them in on nice buses, feed them a catered lunch, and have speakers in a not-inexpensive conference hall, just so that they can understand the big picture of your company?"

Jacob smiled. "Yes, that's about right."

"Why do you do that?"

Arleen added, "To connect them with each other and with the company. For example, we share about what properties and markets we are buying in and how this fits into the overall company strategy. If they each only know their one little piece of the pie, then that's all they're ever going to know. But if they can connect all the pieces together, they are part of a bigger thing— it's one way of helping each team member live a purpose-driven life. It also raises their potential for advancement."

By this time, they had reached the parking lot. "Well, this is where we part company, I guess," Jacob said. "I do hope we've answered all your questions, and that you have a better sense now of how we operate."

"You have, and I do," Elena said. "I still have some thinking to do—I want to sleep on it, really—but I can tell you that you've made a very good impression on me so far!"

"I'm glad," Jacob said, and he opened the door for Arleen, got into his car and drove away.

Gabriel and Elena watched them go and stood for a moment in silence.

Then Gabriel said, "It's way too hot today. I want ice cream. Would you like to get some ice cream with me?"

Elena's heart fluttered in her chest. "I'd love that," she said.

*But it's **not** a date*, she thought.

Chapter 5

Love and Ice Cream

What the heck does he think he's doing? Elena wondered.

And then, aloud, she said, "Why are you getting on the freeway? I thought we were just going to grab some ice cream?"

"We are," Gabriel replied. "But I guess I feel like going downtown. I like people-watching, and I enjoy hanging out in areas where there's a lot of foot traffic and human activity." He smiled at her, and his voice took on a light, self-deprecating tone. "I guess I don't get out much," he admitted.

"I'm not surprised," Elena said. "Raising a kid by yourself must be a big challenge."

"It can be," he said. "How'd you know I was a single dad, anyway?"

"Total recall," she replied, grinning and tapping her temple with an index finger. "I never forget anything. You probably don't remember, but when you first became my patient, I was making small talk while working on your mouth, and I asked if you were married."

"Yikes, I hope that wasn't too awkward a moment for you."

"It happens," she said and then decided to change the subject. She waited a beat and then said, "Thank you for introducing me to the Garzas. I really like them."

"My pleasure," Gabriel replied. "Do you think you'll invest in one of their properties?"

Elena bit her lip and frowned. "I'm leaning toward it, yes, but I really need to sleep on it. I have a bit of a conservative disposition when it comes to making big decisions. This is a new investment we're talking about, and I worked very hard for a very long time to earn my money."

"That's understandable," he replied as the Downtown skyline came into view. A minute later, he exited the freeway, listening to Elena continue to think out loud about a decision he could tell she'd already made. *Funny how the mind works that way*, he thought. *I wonder what other decisions she's already made subconsciously. Or which ones I've made, come to think of it.*

There was a Baskin Robbins at the corner of Euclid and San Pedro avenues, and Gabriel could hardly believe his good fortune in finding a parking spot right in front of it. They went in and ordered two large cones—Peanut Butter 'n Chocolate for him and Vanilla for her. *Wow*, he thought. *She really* does *have a conservative disposition!*

As though she'd heard his thought, she said, mock defensively, "Yeah, it's not an exciting choice, but it's what I like! I'm a vanilla gal."

"No judgment!"

The cashier handed them their cones, and Elena insisted on paying since Gabriel had been nice enough to go to all this trouble to make sure she got sound investment advice.

Gabriel took a couple of steps toward the tables by the window but stopped short when Elena said, "Hey! Where do you think you're going?"

His brow furrowed in confusion. "To sit down?"

"Uh-uh. We're sitting outside!"

"But it's hot out!"

"Exactly! We'll enjoy our cold treats more outside in the heat. That's the whole point of *getting* ice cream on a hot day!"

Gabriel had to admit to himself that he could sort of see her point.

"Better yet," she said, "why don't we take a walk down to the Riverwalk? It's really pretty down there and excellent for people-watching if that's what you're in the mood to do. It's only about a mile!"

Inwardly, Gabriel quailed at the thought of walking a mile on a day like this . . . but he knew it wouldn't do to let Elena see his reluctance. *Besides*, he thought, *who wants to be a killjoy?*

They set out walking southward, but not too briskly, in deference to the heat. "So," Gabriel said, "what factors are you weighing in this big decision?"

"Well," she said, "the soundness of the investment itself is obviously the number one concern—and the Garzas made a pretty airtight case for that in their presentation last night, and I like how they care about their team and their properties. Plus, *you've* invested in a couple of their syndications, and you seem to have done pretty well from it.

"I *have* done very well," Gabriel replied. "They are also very transparent in their reporting. Like clockwork, each month, I get a full set of financial reports. They also detail where they are on the capital projects (CAPEX), including before and after pictures. Very reassuring. My favorite is the narrative that spells out in layman's terms how the property is performing and what to expect in the near future. And it helps me sleep at night, knowing they invest in their properties . . . I know they care."

"The other consideration is *time*," Elena said. "I don't have much of a personal life. I don't date, really, and I don't even have too many friends. No social life and not too many hobbies anymore. My whole life is work, work, work. I'm tired of living that way, and I'd like to be able to scale back my practice a little bit. Maybe open at nine o'clock in the morning rather than eight and close the office on Saturdays. Maybe take a vacation once in a while. But to do that, I'd need a reliable passive income."

"That was one of my own motivations as well," Gabriel said. "After my wife passed away, I threw myself into my work in order to avoid dealing with it—and also to maximize my ability to provide for my son now that he was half-orphaned.

"But after a while, I began to realize that working myself half to death wasn't making me a better father. Just the opposite, in fact. I was missing out on Tony's life. He learned to tie his shoes, and it was the babysitter he showed off for. He lost his first baby tooth, and it was the babysitter who found it when it disappeared into the couch cushions. And it was the babysitter who played tooth-fairy and put a quarter under his pillow that night. Heck, I guess I'm lucky I learned about that tooth before *you* did!

"I knew I needed to be more present in Tony's life, or I was going to miss it. I knew he needed me around. That meant I couldn't keep working sixteen-hour days running one tech start-up after another. So, like you, I thought of real estate. And like you, I had a friend who recommended the Garzas.

"Anyway, the point is I get it. I can relate to where you're coming from." He chuckled ruefully. "And I guess we're alike in other ways—I don't date much either!"

They walked in silence for a minute, during which time they finished their ice cream and arrived at the river. They walked down the steps, from street level down to the riverside promenade for which San Antonio is famous. Finding a park bench, they sat together and watched the river flow by them.

Elena thought hard about everything they'd talked about that day and about the impression Jacob and Arleen had made on her over the past twenty-four hours. She still felt a reflexive nervousness about committing to an investment model that was so unfamiliar to her . . . but she realized she was running out of reasons not to move on it.

Chapter 6

A Leap of Faith

The next day was Sunday—Elena's only day off—so she and Gabriel spent the day together. Gabriel brought Tony with him, and the three of them had lunch, followed by another trip to another ice cream parlor, as Gabriel felt guilty about having gone for ice cream without his son the day before. Then they went to the movies, after which Gabriel dropped Tony off at Jill's place so that he and Elena could have dinner together alone.

At around ten o'clock, Gabriel's black 1975 911 Carrera pulled up and parked in front of Elena's house, and he got out to walk her to her door.

They stood at the door, holding hands and gazing into each other's eyes. "Thank you for dinner, Gabe," Elena said.

Gabriel laughed. "So it's 'Gabe, now, is it? No, really, though . . . thank *you*."

"What for?"

"For waking me up when I didn't even know I was asleep. I haven't felt this happy in seven years, and I owe it to you."

Elena smiled. "And to think we both owe our happiness to something as unromantic as a real estate investment!"

They laughed together over this, and then Gabriel said, "Speaking of which . . . have you made a decision about that?"

Elena let out a deep sigh and then was silent for a few seconds. Finally, she said, "I don't know. The Garzas seem like awfully nice people, and I get a good, honest vibe from them. But you never can tell, can you? There have been times in the past when I've been let down by people I trusted. People I thought I had vetted pretty well. I mean, I'm sure that kind of thing happens to everybody eventually, but it's made me circumspect. Like I've said, I have a bit of a cautious, conservative disposition—"

Gabriel interjected, "Really, Miss Vanilla Ice Cream? You don't say!"

Elena laughed. "Tony was really appalled by that!"

"Especially when I told him it was the same thing you had yesterday!"

"Anyway," she said, "returning to my point, I'm very wary, very cautious about romance. And you're right; I do blame that on my work more than I should. I'm the same way about my money.

"But yesterday, I threw caution to the winds when it came to *you* because I feel like I can trust you. So, I trust you . . . and you, in turn, trust Jacob and Arleen Garza. Plus, everything they've told me about their business model and meeting their team inspires confidence. In fact, it's almost *too* good to be true, which makes me nervous.

"But you trust them, and I trust *you*. So yes, as soon as they find a property that looks right . . . I'm in."

* * *

Monday morning came too soon, it seemed. Elena wished she could have had another whole day off to spend with her new friend. But duty called, and she had patients who were counting on her. Still, even the daily grind of her commute to her office couldn't dim her spirits, and she practically floated through her workday.

When she got home, she checked her e-mail and found that she had a message from the Garzas. Opening it, she saw the REEP Equity logo, followed by some news that made her heart race:

Elena,

We're writing to you today to inform you of an opportunity to invest with us in Desmond Gardens, an apartment complex in San Antonio's Beacon Hill neighborhood. For this purpose, we have secured advantageous financing with interest-only payments until 2030!

To some investors, a deal like this sounds too good to be true, and some have asked how we were able to get such a great loan. In today's market, loan assumptions are extremely advantageous, especially when we can get terms such as the ones we have secured in Desmond Gardens! We can assure you that REEP's relationships, experience, and knowledge have all culminated together to allow us to acquire an asset like Desmond Gardens with this great loan. Below, we go into more detail and why you don't want to miss out on this investment opportunity!

Below this was a chart that clarified the timeline of the sale, the terms of the loan, and other such information. Elena skimmed this, promising herself she'd read it more carefully when she'd calmed down.

As you'll see, we are closing on the property next month but keeping (or "assuming") the current loan in place of Desmond Gardens. Even better, when we go to sell the property, the loan is still assumable by the next buyer, with the same fixed rate for the remaining term of the loan! Not only is REEP set up for success on this acquisition, but our exit strategies are more flexible and attractive to Buyers when we look to sell Desmond Gardens. And, as always, Arleen and I will be investing our own funds into the purchase of Desmond Gardens.

We hope you will join us, but in the meantime, please reach out with any questions at invest@reepequity.com.

Our Very Best,
Jacob & Arleen Garza
REEP Equity

Below the signature was a list of the property's features—its occupancy rate, local home values, etc.—and its amenities. Beneath that was a series of beautiful photos.

Well, Elena thought, I've already made one leap of faith this week. Now it's time to make another.

She clicked "Reply" and began typing:

Jacob and Arleen,

This sounds like a wonderful opportunity, and I am very much interested! Please let me know as soon as possible what my next steps should be.

–Elena Madsen, DDS

After clicking "Send," Elena leaned back in her chair and took a moment to savor the feeling of immense satisfaction and relief that suddenly washed over her. Gone was the cloud of indecision that had hung over her, along with the anxiety that had flowed from that indecision. In place of those negative emotions was an almost giddy sense of excitement.

That excitement stayed with her for the remainder of the evening. When bedtime came, she thought about the e-mail while she showered and brushed her teeth; she could hardly imagine how she would be able to get to sleep. And yet, when she finally laid her head on the pillow, she fell within moments into a deeper and more relaxing sleep than she had managed to achieve in years.

The next morning, her eyes had no sooner opened than she found herself reaching for her phone to check her e-mail. It was early, but she already had a reply from Arleen:

Hi Elena!

We'll be holding a webinar this coming Saturday, during which we will provide granular details about this investment, with a Q&A to follow.

Here is a link to the webinar URL. At the end of the presentation, after the Q&A, you'll be able to make your investment by clicking a link or scanning a QR code.

Hope to see you there!

Arleen

That's only four days from now, Elena thought. *I can hardly wait!*

* * *

That Saturday, at 9:59, Elena sat at her computer, opened her e-mail, clicked on the link Arleen had sent, and logged on.

Onscreen were Jacob and Arleen, sitting together behind a desk. "Good morning!" Jacob said. "And welcome. Today, we'll be telling you about Desmond Gardens and why we think it's a great investment opportunity for you."

He went on to explain that the webinar was being recorded and that if participants missed anything, they'd be able to view the recording later. He also informed everyone that there would be a Q&A at the end of the presentation and directed their attention to a link in a chat box if anyone wanted to make their commitment at any time during the webinar. "We take commitments on a first-come, first-served basis," he explained.

After presenting a brief legal disclaimer, Jacob proceeded to expand on his introduction. "A little bit about us: I was a career software guy in Dallas and started my first company when I was twenty-six. I sold my last one in 2007, and we moved to San Antonio. That's when we bought our first twenty-four-unit apartment complex."

Arleen picked up the thread: "I have a degree in finance, and I'm sharing that in order to let you know that I'm a numbers gal. I really like the numbers side of this business, so the acquisitions piece works very well for me. I'm a former Bank of America executive, and I was in banking for twenty years. I was a lender, I managed banking centers, and I led a nationwide marketing team. This background allowed me to pick up a set of highly relevant skills that I've brought with me to REEP. We are both certified apartment managers and certified apartment portfolio supervisors through the National Apartment Association."

Elena was mesmerized. She realized, suddenly, that there was a lot she hadn't known about the Garzas. She knew they seemed like nice, smart people and seemed to have a lot of experience in their field—but knowing the exact nature of that experience, as she now did, gave her even more confidence.

The event went on for about an hour. They showed photos of Desmond Gardens—photos so pretty that Elena wished for a moment that she lived there. They described how various aspects of the neighborhood had influenced their selection of this particular property—low crime rate, proximity to freeways, schools, and shopping centers, et cetera. They talked about the impressive tax benefits of multi-family investments (a subject that had not even occurred to Elena) and about the various factors that were driving the increase in the market price of rent in the area. Near the end, they talked about the improvements they planned to make to the property and the surprising ways in which some of those improvements would increase the value of everyone's initial investment.

Throughout the presentation, they showed slides that Elena found very helpful for conceptualizing and internalizing everything they were talking about. There were diagrams and photos. There were bullet lists outlining the size range of the units, the average square footage of both the one-bedroom and two-bedroom apartments, the amenities (including full-size in-unit washer/dryer connections), and more. Additional slides clarified the financial aspects of the deal, while Jacob and Arleen carefully explained what the numbers meant.

Elena was impressed—not just with Desmond Gardens itself or the apparent soundness of the deal but also with the exhaustive attention the Garzas paid to transparency and thoroughness. She knew there were a lot of fly-by-night real estate operations out there . . . and this was clearly not one of them.

"I believe that concludes the webinar," Jacob said at last. "So now we can go to questions and answers."

Elena's phone buzzed, announcing an incoming text message. Arleen was reading out a question someone had asked about occupancy percentages, a subject Elena wasn't especially concerned about, so she opted to take a moment to see who had sent the text.

The screen showed a message from Jimmy, her receptionist. (Elena had rescheduled a few Saturday morning appointments, but her office was open that day, and her hygienist, Elizabeth, was doing cleanings.)

Jimmy's text read:

911. Mrs. Park is here, no appointment, but she says she's in severe pain and can't wait to see you. What should I do?

Momentarily flustered, Elena forgot that Jacob had said at the outset that the webinar was being recorded, and so she found herself dividing her attention.

Having finished with the occupancy question, Arleen was now answering another participant's question, this one about insurance. ". . . and that's why we carry lots of insurance. So, from an investor standpoint, people can feel very comfortable that their investment is protected, just like their home might be . . ."

Distracted, Elena didn't quite hear her. She began to feel anxious—this webinar was important to her; she wondered, could Mrs. Park wait a few more minutes? In her mind, concern wrestled with annoyance. Elena had warned the lady that an abscess might develop if she didn't take her advice . . .

"So, insurance covers the lost rents," Arleen continued, and they do it quickly, so the distributions keep going . . ."

Elena's phone buzzed again with another text from Jimmy:

Benny not here with her. This is bad.

"Benny," Elena knew, was Mrs. Park's grandson, Benedict. Benny usually accompanied his grandmother to her dental appointments to translate for her since her English wasn't particularly fluent. The fact that she'd come without him said volumes about how much pain she must be in. There was probably one heck of a crisis at her reception desk right now, as Elena doubted that Mrs. Park's English was good enough for her staff to communicate clearly when she'd be back.

". . . so you never need to worry!" Arleen's voice went up a little at the end of that last sentence in a way that signaled to Elena that she'd finished speaking. *Uh-oh*, she thought. *I just missed everything she said for the last minute and a half. I hope it wasn't important.*

She hurriedly tapped out a reply to Jimmy:

"On my way. Will call you in 5 min."

Her concern for poor Mrs. Park had finally won out over her irritation that yet another patient who disregarded her advice was encroaching on the small slice of non-work time she had each week. And amid her anxiety over her patient's suffering, she forgot all about her uneasy feeling that she'd possibly missed something important that Arleen had said.

Mrs. Park's abscess took an hour or so to deal with, pushing back other patients' appointments and throwing Elena's whole day out of whack. By the time she got home, all she could think about was finishing what she'd started that morning with the Garzas. In her inbox, she found another e-mail from them, this one with the link to the recording of the webinar and instructions on how to complete her commitment to Desmond Gardens. When she'd finished filling out the short subscription form, she sat back with a sense of deep satisfaction that soothed her after her difficult, frustrating day, almost like taking a nice, hot bath might have done.

As soon as that thought occurred to her, she decided that a bath would, in fact, be a wonderful way to celebrate the day's accomplishment, so she went to the bathroom to begin running one.

* * *

Two months later, Elena found herself almost unable to believe how well her life was going. She and Gabriel had also made some new friends over the past couple of months. Gabriel and Jacob had really hit it off, and the four of them now occasionally went to dinner together. They weren't *super* close, but they really enjoyed one another's company. Given the impoverishment of Elena's social life over the course of the past decade, making new friends was like coming to an oasis in the desert.

She was ruminating on those very thoughts one afternoon on her way home from work when her phone rang. Seeing that it was

Gabriel, she pressed a button on her dashboard to take the call on the car's speakers. "Hi, Gabe," she said.

"Good news," Gabriel said. "I just got a call from Jacob. The deal went through. Desmond Gardens is now in the hands of the Garzas 'management company."

Elena squealed with delight so loudly that Gabriel had to hold the phone away from his ear.

"Anyway," he said, "they've invited us to dinner, so put on your dancing shoes. Tonight, we're celebrating."

Elena snorted derisively. "Dancing shoes?"

Gabriel sighed. "Figure of speech."

"I can't dance to save my life, and neither can you!"

"Don't be pedantic," Gabriel said. "Just pick out something nice to wear, and I'll pick you up at eight."

* * *

Jacob suggested that Gabriel and Elena should pick the restaurant, so Gabriel gave them directions to his favorite downtown sushi joint. When they arrived, they found Jacob and Arleen already seated at a table, waiting for them.

"Have a seat," Jacob said as Gabriel and Elena slid into the booth. "I hope this table is okay with you."

"Normally, I like to sit at the bar to have sushi," Gabriel said, "but for a party of four, a table is better! We can all see one another's faces."

The waiter arrived and brought them menus, and while they were discussing their options, Jacob's phone buzzed to alert him to a text. "Sorry about that," he said. "I'll turn the ringer off."

But when he pulled the phone from his pocket and looked at it, his face suddenly contorted into a frown. "Excuse me," he said, "I have to deal with this. I'm sorry." And with that, he got up, walked to the door, and stepped outside.

"Oh my," Elena said. "That looked ominous. I hope everything is okay."

"I'm sure it is," Arleen said. "But you know how it is, running a business. You're in the middle of something personal, and suddenly your phone buzzes and something urgent takes you right out of whatever you're doing."

"Hah! I know *exactly* how that is," Elena replied, thinking about how Mrs. Park's abscess had interrupted and distracted her a couple of months before.

All of a sudden, however, she felt uneasy. It wasn't like Jacob to just get up and walk away from a table like that. *Was* something wrong?

The three of them studied their menus in silence for a minute, and then Jacob returned. The mood at the table had been festive . . . but now Elena saw a grave expression on Jacob's face.

"What's the matter, sweetheart?" Arleen said as he sat down.

For a moment, Jacob merely stared at the table without answering. Then, speaking slowly, he said, "It's Desmond Gardens. There's been a fire."

A hush fell over the table, and suddenly, Elena began to hyperventilate.

Jacob frowned. "Elena," he said, "are you okay?"

"Yeah, honey," Gabriel said. "What's the matter?"

"'What's the *matter*?'" Elena asked, incredulous. "That . . . that was a lot of money, and now it's all burned up, and you say, 'What's the matter?'"

Jacob said. "Everything's okay, really! The fire wasn't that bad, only affecting a few apartments. No one was hurt, thank God. And your investment—*our* investment—is completely safe."

Elena began to get herself under control. Tentatively, she began to speak. "Our money is . . . safe? Really?"

"Of course it is!" Arleen said. "Didn't you attend the webinar? We talked about this. Everything is insured. The residents are required to have renter's insurance, and we have property and casualty insurance, which includes a *loss of revenue* coverage for any lost rent. You and Gabriel have absolutely nothing to worry about, I promise you!"

Elena felt a wave of embarrassment wash over her. "I'm sorry," she said. "I've behaved foolishly."

"Don't give it another thought," Arleen replied. "You take your investments seriously, and that makes it scary when something like this happens. But I can assure you there's nothing to fear."

"How bad *was* the fire?" Gabriel asked.

"Well, I don't yet know everything there is to know," Jacob said. "But from what I just now learned in that brief phone call, it wasn't too terrible. Seems a young tenant left a dish towel on the stove. This is not surprising since most apartment fires start in the kitchen. No one was injured, and it was mostly contained to a single unit, with some smoke damage to a few adjoining ones, I think. Our team is on site and arranging for residents to stay in a hotel or our model unit until morning when we can make more concrete arrangements for them. I'll go by later and inspect it in person."

"So, how bad do you think the damage might be?" Elena asked.

"Well, in my experience, besides whatever was burned and whatever smoke damage may have occurred, there'll be some water damage. But again, nothing insurance won't cover."

Elena suddenly thought about what it must be like to have to live in a place that had been scarred in that way. "And where will the people in the damaged apartments go?" she asked.

"We're going to take care of them," Arleen said firmly. "We have a seasoned team, with insurance experts and procedures in place, and we're going to follow them. We have a handful of vacant units in other buildings we own, and we'll move those residents into those units while their own apartment homes are being repaired."

"Our team is very capable," Jacob said, "but I don't think I will enjoy dinner until I lay eyes on the damage myself. Can we take a rain check?"

"Of course," Gabriel said.

After the Garzas had left the table, Elena said, "Gabriel, I'm embarrassed at my behavior. I'm so sorry. I can't imagine what you must think of me. I'm not usually prone to that kind of panicky overreaction."

"Don't give it another thought," Gabriel said. "Do you still want to stay for dinner, or should we call it a night?"

"I'm still hungry," Elena replied. "So, let's stay."

She paused a moment and then added, "And let's consider this a date!"

Chapter 7

The Aftermath of the Fire

Elena parked her car and stared across the darkened street. It was well after midnight, and the activity surrounding Desmond Gardens made it hard to make out what, exactly, was going on over there.

She and Gabriel had left the sushi bar at around ten o'clock, and Gabriel had brought her straight home, walked her to her door, kissed her good night, and gone home himself. At eleven o'clock, she'd gone to bed . . . and found herself lying awake, unable to set her mind at rest.

How bad had that fire been? Jacob clearly wasn't worried about it, and all the consequences of the fire clearly had either been dealt with ahead of time (insurance would cover any losses incurred by the investors or the tenants) or were being dealt with right now by the Garzas and their team.

On the other hand, she thought, the fire clearly hadn't been completely *trivial,* either, or Jacob wouldn't have felt the need to leave the dinner table to go see it for himself. And the longer she lay there, trying futilely to sleep, the clearer it became that sleep would not come until she, too, saw the situation with her own eyes.

Now, she found herself sitting uneasily in her car, parked across the street from Desmond Gardens, wondering what to do next—wondering what she was even looking for or trying to learn here. Although the scene was illuminated by streetlamps, it was still fairly dark, and the flashing lights of the firetrucks and police cars made it hard for her to focus on anything at this distance.

There was a crowd milling about in front of the building, most likely a mixture of Desmond Gardens residents and curious passers-by, in addition to the uniformed firemen walking to and fro, going about whatever their duties were. At either end of the block, the sidewalk was blocked by traffic cones and yellow police tape.

The flashing lights and streetlamps threw a dark shadow beside one of the firetrucks, and standing in that shadow were a number of men in suits having what looked like a very important conversation. One of the men appeared to be about Jacob's size and was wearing a suit that resembled his, but at this distance, in this light, she couldn't be sure it was him.

She quickly realized that if she were going to learn anything, she would have to get out of her car and approach the scene. The thought of doing so made her nervous, however. She was still embarrassed by her behavior at dinner, and the last thing she wanted was for Jacob and Arleen to see her there late at night playing Nancy Drew when she should have been in bed, sleeping the tranquil sleep of someone who knows her investments are secure. Of course, the Garzas were too kind to pass judgment on her, but she respected them and didn't want them to think she was some kind of nervous, neurotic ninny.

And frankly, she was starting to *feel* like one. Nevertheless, she felt that she had to know what had happened and what would happen next.

Elena reached into the glove compartment and grabbed the Houston Astros ballcap that she kept there for exceptionally sunny days. She put it on, pulled her hair into a ponytail, and stuffed it under the hat. She was wearing different clothes than she'd worn at dinner, which she figured would also help her avoid being recognized.

And if they do spot me, so what? she thought. *I'll just fess up to being nervous and unable to sleep, and they'll pat me on the head and tell me to go home and not worry.*

*I'd rather **not** admit to that, though, because I know this **is** foolish, and I **should** be home asleep. And besides, they've got enough on their plate tonight without me distracting them. So, I'll keep my head down.*

Confident in her disguise, Elena got out of her car and moved toward the curious crowd that was hanging around outside the building. She sidled over to the front of the fire truck where she'd seen those men talking and got as close as she could to eavesdrop on their conversation.

"—just glad that everyone is okay. The important thing here is that everyone is safe." Recognizing Jacob's voice, Elena patted herself on the back for having correctly surmised that he was one of the men she'd spotted earlier.

"Agreed," said another voice, "although we'll still have to conduct our own investigation in coordination with the fire department. Jorge, do you have an estimate of how much longer it'll be before you can let me in there to start doing my job?"

"I don't know, Tim," Jorge replied. Elena guessed he had to be some sort of fire department official or team captain or something like that. "Hard to say, exactly. I'd give it maybe another hour or so."

"That's fine," Tim said. *And he must be an insurance adjustor,* Elena thought.

"What about my team, Jorge?" Jacob said. "They're standing around waiting, and I'd like to get them in there to start with debris cleanup as soon as possible. When you let Tim in there, can they go too?"

"Okay with me," Jorge replied.

"Actually, Jacob, if you don't mind, I'd like to have an hour to myself in there before you start cleaning up," Tim said. "Otherwise, my job is harder, and I might miss something."

"I understand," Jacob said. "I guess, worst-case scenario, I end up sending them home tonight and starting cleanup first thing in the morning. We can assume we're covered, though, right?"

"I don't see how you wouldn't be," Tim replied. "Understand that I can't make any definitive statements until I've done my job, of course . . . but unless I find that it was arson, then everything should be fine."

Jorge said. "My boys tell me it looks like an ordinary, run-of-the-mill kitchen stove fire caused by negligence on the part of a resident."

"Yeah, I know," Tim replied. "You said that before, and I believe you. I still gotta do my job and check off all the formal-process boxes, though."

"Speaking of that resident," Jacob said, "How is she? I was told she's okay, but that's all I know."

Jorge smiled. "I wouldn't worry," he said. "The EMTs took her away before you got here, but I spoke to one of them before they left. She's got some mild smoke-inhalation injuries and a nasty second-degree burn on her hand from trying to put the fire out while she was in a full-blown panic. But from the sound of it, I'd guess she'll be home tomorrow."

Jacob sighed ruefully. "Yeah, which means that before then, I need to make sure she has a 'home' to go to."

"What are you going to do?"

"We have another complex on Starcrest Drive that has a few empty units," Jacob said. The team has already spoken to the tenants in the other two units that had the smoke damage. Tomorrow morning, she'll call a moving company and have all their stuff brought there."

From her hiding place on the other side of the truck, Elena couldn't see what was going on where the three men were talking, so she was startled when she suddenly heard a woman's voice say, "Good thing the fire department's here, 'cause my ears are burning!"

"There you are!" Jacob said, his voice bright with surprise, and Elena realized that Arleen must have walked up behind them.

"Nice to see you again, Mrs. Garza," said Tim. "Sorry, we're not meeting under better circumstances."

"Me too," Arleen said, her voice heavy with fatigue.

"Jacob was just telling us that you've got places for these people who got burned out of their homes?"

"Yes, we have a building on Starcrest Drive with a few vacant apartments. For tonight, I've got them sorted out with hotel rooms—except for the girl in the hospital, poor thing—and tomorrow, we'll take care of moving them all into their temporary new homes."

"They may be in those temporary homes for a while," Jorge said. "Those apartments in there look pretty ugly right now. Rebuilding and repairing everything will be an expensive head-ßache. I don't envy you."

"I'm not worried," Jacob said. "Unless Tim finds out I torched the place myself; insurance should cover everything, including even our own lost income—if there is any."

"Besides," Arleen said, "you don't spend over a decade in the real estate business without befriending a few contractors. We'll get a fair deal, and we'll make sure the work gets done quickly. I've already spoken to Rachel at Stone Family Construction, and they're sending a guy tomorrow to inspect the apartments and give us an estimate."

"Two of those apartments appear to only have smoke damage," Jorge said. "So, you may get away with just having to paint them. The other one, though, the place where the fire started . . . well, you'll have your work cut out for you."

Jacob waved his hand dismissively. "It'll all get taken care of. We were planning on doing some renovations and improvements anyway to improve the value of the complex. Again, no one was seriously injured, and that's the important thing."

Elena couldn't help but smile, marveling at the methodical organization and efficiency of the Garzas' response to this disaster. In fact, she realized *disaster* wasn't really the right word. If this fire had happened at some other building, one operated by some indifferent third-party management company, it very well *could* have been a disaster—for the property owners and the residents.

But it wasn't. The residents of the smoke-damaged apartments were already resting comfortably in nice hotel rooms. And tomorrow, they—along with the woman in the hospital—would be headed to new apartments in a different building, where they would stay until their homes were repaired. In the meantime, the teams had spoken to them and reassured them that all would be well, so they would rest easy tonight despite the traumatic evening they'd had. The insurance matter would be sorted out promptly, and the debris cleanup would begin within an hour or two or by tomorrow at the latest. The Garzas' contacts in the construction business would get started on the necessary repairs within a matter of days, and before too long, it would be almost as though nothing had happened at all.

As far as Elena could see, the only people who would suffer any serious discomfort in the coming days would be the lady in the hospital, whose burn would take a while to heal, and the Garzas themselves, who would get little sleep tonight and had a day of daunting tasks ahead of them tomorrow.

Once again, she blushed with shame at her panicky overreaction at dinner. There had never been any cause for alarm. These people, the residents of Desmond Gardens, were in good hands.

And so were she and Gabriel.

Keeping her head down, Elena made her way back to her car, drove home, and got the best night's sleep she'd had in months.

Epilogue

"Ouch!"

Elena dropped the hot cookie sheet she'd just picked up, letting it clatter on the oven rack, and ran to the sink to run cold water on her burned fingers, cursing her carelessness. When the pain subsided after a few seconds, she shut the water off and examined her fingertips. They were bright red, but they looked like they'd be fine by tomorrow.

Despite the unwelcome adrenaline rush from the little injury, her good mood remained unshaken. It had been a year since the fire at Desmond Gardens, and these days she was just happy to have *time* for this kind of activity. It had not always been so, as she well remembered.

Of course, cookie-baking had always been part of her routine—her *work* routine. As Gabriel had noticed on the day they'd gone for that fateful non-date at the coffee shop, Elena deemed it good business for her office to smell of chocolate chip happiness. But now, the time she spent baking cookies felt more like leisure time than work, and she looked forward to Gabriel's arrival later that afternoon, knowing he would be eager for his share of them.

She put on a pair of oven mitts and returned to the task of extricating her cookies from the oven, glancing at the clock as she did so. It was 5:08; Gabriel would probably be here within a half hour, if not sooner.

The Garzas had invited them both on an investor bus tour of Desmond Gardens so that the investors could see first-hand the $2 million renovation project that would increase the value of their investments. Elena had regretfully declined—she needed a quiet day at home, and these cookies weren't going to bake themselves. But Gabriel had taken them up on their offer. He was endlessly curious and loved to look at those kinds of things.

Elena, on the other hand, was more sanguine. Thanks to the Garzas' regular newsletter e-mails, she knew the work had been done, and she had absolute faith that it had been done well. She had faith in her investment, and while she appreciated the transparency the bus tour represented, she felt no need to take time out of her tranquil Saturday.

She smiled, reflecting that she had not always been so mellow. Her journey over the past year and a half had not been the same as Gabriel's. In the days when they had first "upgraded" their relationship from a *doctor-patient* to *friends* to a *romantic couple*, she had been overworked and prone to stress, especially where money was concerned.

Placing her sheet of cookies on the counter to cool, she turned back toward the stove, where a pot of water was finally coming to a boil. She was multitasking, cooking dinner for herself and Gabriel while she baked cookies for her patients (and Gabriel!). She grabbed a box of rotini from the cabinet and dumped it all into the pot, still marveling at what a different woman she was today compared to who she'd been a year ago.

Gabriel had been the easygoing yin to her tense, nervous yang. But she wasn't tense and nervous by nature; she'd just allowed herself to get that way. She'd been worried about her retirement, remembering how her grandfather had started planning too late for his and had been forced to come live with her and her mother in his late autumn years.

But Gabriel had always been effortlessly calm and good-humored—and he'd had every reason to be. His financial picture was secure, and he'd reached a point where money was never again going to be something he had to worry about. At the time they'd met, however, she hadn't yet reached that point, and this state of affairs had made her perpetually anxious.

She finished stirring her pasta into the water and turned her attention to her sauce, dipping her wooden spoon into it for a taste. With regret, she realized dinner wouldn't be ready before Gabriel arrived.

It occurred to her that part of the reason for the difference in their temperament at the time was that Gabriel already knew the Garzas and had already been invested with them. Passive multifamily real-estate investment had been a whole new world for her, and she'd found it intimidating and scary. *The unknown is* always *scary*, she thought, adding a little more chopped basil to the sauce.

But it hadn't been unknown to Gabriel, and thanks to his guidance (as well as Jacob and Arleen's, of course), it hadn't remained unknown or scary to her for very long. As the months had gone by, she'd seen one thing after another that had put her mind at ease. The transparent reporting on every development that occurred had reassured her. REEP clearly wasn't some fly-by-night operation, and the professionalism of their e-mails and other communications had been nothing short of exemplary.

Gabriel had already seen all of this when she'd met him, but she'd had to see it all for herself and come independently to her own state of confidence. *I guess no one can take your journey for you*, she thought, giving her still-simmering sauce another taste and lowering the flame a bit.

The distributions, when they started coming, had been thrilling. Of course, she knew she'd had to put money *into* the machine in order to get money *out* of it . . . and yet when those distributions came, they still somehow seemed like magic, like free money suddenly appearing out of nowhere.

More than any of that, though, the biggest reason for her newfound peace of mind was that the holistic, big picture of her financial future was improving right before her eyes. She could see her retirement taking shape, and she realized that these passive real estate investments were the perfect vehicle for that future. Her only regret was that she hadn't done it sooner. ("Everybody, including me, says that," Jacob told her.)

And because of that, she was now about to invest in yet another REEP apartment complex.

While she was thinking about these things, her hands had been operating on autopilot, stirring the sauce. Lifting the spoon to her lips, she tasted it again now and judged it to have reached perfection. Glancing at the clock, she saw that it was now 5:16— time to drain the pasta. She turned off the flame on both burners and dumped her pasta water into a colander she'd placed in the sink. And as she was doing so, there came a knock at the front door.

"It's open!" she shouted, knowing exactly who it was. *Looks like dinner's going to be right on time, even though he's a little early,* she thought with pleasure. She heard Gabriel's footsteps approaching the kitchen and turned her head to greet him with a kiss, her hands still engaged in her culinary labors.

"Hi honey," he said. "Miss me?"

Elena laughed. "You dropped by this morning just before you left, so it's only been a few hours! So no, I haven't missed you!"

Gabriel feigned dismay, as he always did when she teased him. He was good at it, she thought. He really did look crestfallen.

"How was the tour?" she asked.

"I'll tell you in a minute," he said. "Gotta hit the powder room!"

"Then be sure to wash your hands well," she said. "I'll have dinner on the table by the time you get back."

When Gabriel finished his ablutions and emerged, he saw that Elena was as good as her word: she'd set the table earlier, and now it was graced with pasta, Caesar salad, and a bottle of Shiraz.

"Oh my, that smells good," Gabriel said. "I'm famished!"

"Then sit down and dig in," Elena replied, "and tell me about your day."

"Well," he said, sitting down and picking up his utensils, "Arleen and Jacob say hello, and they're sorry they didn't get to see you. And I got to meet their adult children, Victoria and Jack."

"Really? What were they like?"

"They seemed nice, although we didn't get a chance to talk for very long. They were pretty busy. Really, the interesting thing about meeting them was what it made me think about." He took a bite of his pasta and moaned with uninhibited delight. "Wow, this is good!"

"Thank you, but don't get distracted. You were saying about the Garza children?"

"Well, just their presence there, along with Arleen and Jacob, as a family unit . . . it said something to me. It said that this is a family business . . . a *legacy* business. And people involved in those kinds of businesses tend to take them very seriously. These aren't people who are just out to make a quick buck—not that I ever thought they were, mind you. But seeing them working together as a family . . . I guess it just brought that all home for me in a way that hadn't hit me before, you know?"

"Yeah, I think I know what you mean. How did the complex look? Did you get a chance to see the units that burned last year?"

"Only one unit burned," he reminded her. "The others just had some smoke damage. Anyway, no, we weren't taken into those units—they're occupied. Remember, they all had people living in them before the fire, and now that the place is all fixed up and renovated, those people are back in their old homes."

"I guess that makes sense," Elena said. What about Desmond Gardens as a whole, though? Does it look very different?"

"In some ways, yeah," Gabriel replied. "I mean, of course, it's still the same place. But in a lot of ways, yes, it's very different! Lots of amenities that weren't there before. New paint job on the exterior. New and better-looking patio fences separating the exterior portions of the units."

"Really? I thought those fences looked nice enough before."

"They were fine, I guess," he said. "But you should see the new ones. Everything that was nice is now nicer. I mean, most of it was fairly nice before, sure. But Desmond Gardens was built in 1991, and while it's been very well maintained, it's never been upgraded until now."

"I guess that was what Arleen found attractive about it when she first saw it," Elena said. "It was *decent* but ripe for renovation to make it *better*—kind of the sweet spot for acquisition, I suppose. A diamond in the rough."

"Yeah, that's what makes a deal like this lucrative. I think they spent something like two million on it, and you can really see where it went. New washing machines in the laundry facilities and new flooring in some units. They resurfaced the pool and redid the deck. It all looks so lovely. I almost wish I lived there myself!"

Elena took a sip of her wine while another question formed in her mind. "The last time I spoke to Arleen, she mentioned something about new features that would drive up our income from the complex. Did you see anything like that?"

"Yes, I did," Gabriel replied. "The parking lot now has a Reserved section that some residents pay extra for. And on the tour, we learned that they've now instituted pet fees. They also provide smart locks, thermostat technology, and package lockers for things like Amazon deliveries."

"Wow, that's quite an upgrade," Elena said. "It's going to be quite a nice payday when the building is finally sold. Heck, I can hardly wrap my head around the difference it's *already* made in my life."

"You mean your peace-of-mind issues? Yeah, I've seen the change in you over the past few months." He laughed. "When we met, I thought you needed to see a therapist!"

Elena giggled. "I guess I was a little bit neurotic at the time. But I had a lot on my mind, you know? A lot to worry about. A few years ago, I went on Facebook and looked up an old friend from dental school . . . but he wasn't a dentist anymore. In fact, he was destitute and living with his mother."

"Yikes! How did that happen?"

"Just a stupid thing. The kind of stupid thing that can happen to anyone. He had a roller-skating accident, of all things. Damaged his hands so badly that he couldn't hold instruments anymore. Also fell on his face in a way that cost him about 70 percent of his vision."

"Geez, that's awful," Gabriel said.

"Sure was," Elena agreed. "And it got me thinking about *my* future and my retirement. Not just whether I'd be able to retire—that was never really in doubt—but what I'd do if something awful happened to me and I couldn't work anymore. How would I be made whole again? Desmond Gardens got me pointed in the direction of making sure I'll be okay, no matter what. And Villa Elena is going to give me another big push in that direction."

Gabriel's brow furrowed. "What's Villa Elena?"

Elena smiled. "I guess you haven't checked your e-mail this morning. Villa Elena—the name is just a fun coincidence, by the way—is an apartment complex in Houston that REEP is looking into buying."

She stood and began to clear their now-empty dishes. When Gabriel got up to help, she waved him back into his seat. "I'll clean up. Get your phone out and check your e-mail. I'll think you'll probably want in on this one, too."

Gabriel did as he was told, reaching into his pocket for his phone. And when Elena had left the room, he reached into it again and brought out a small box, which he placed in his lap.

A minute later, Elena returned from the kitchen and saw that Gabriel had poured each of them a second glass of wine. "Ooh, living dangerously tonight?"

"Gabriel smiled. "Maybe," he said. "And maybe I've got something I want us to celebrate."

Elena raised an eyebrow. "Do tell?"

"Well, first of all, you're right—this Villa Elena *does* look like something I want to invest in." He paused. "Something I want *us* to invest in."

Elena chucked. "I already told you I'm in on this one!"

"No, not you and me," Gabriel said. "*Us.* Now that your future is secured in a way that you're satisfied with, I want *us* to make investments. Together." He took the little box from his lap, placed it on the table, and opened it.

Inside it was a ring.

"Elena Madsen," Gabriel said, "will you marry me?"

Elena gasped and found that she could hardly catch her breath. For several long, agonizing seconds, she said nothing at all.

Gabriel began to feel nervous and wondered whether he'd miscalculated. "Well . . .?"

Elena finally found her voice and squealed with delight.

She said simply, "It's a date!"

An Invitation to Take Action

We hope you enjoyed the story you've just read—and if you found Elena's or Gabriel's investment concerns relatable and personally compelling, then perhaps we should talk.

This story is a work of fiction, but everything in it is based on how we actually do business. Like its fictional counterpart, the real-life REEP does have an in-house management company that takes care of the properties we purchase with the help of investors like you. And that really does make all the difference in the long-term value of any investment you make with us.

Our investors typically stay with us for up to four years. They receive regular disbursements of their share of the rent from the complex they have invested in. When we sell, the return on their investment can be as high as 65—and in the case of some deals, even higher, as much as 217 percent historically.

Passive vs. Active Investment

When it comes to real estate, you're either a passive investor or an active one. If you're an active investor, then it falls to you to manage the property. You and you alone are responsible not just for collecting rent but also for routine maintenance: replacing old water heaters, unclogging toilets, painting units when there is a change of occupancy, et cetera. Whenever a problem arises with the property, it is your responsibility to fix it or to hire someone to do it for you.

This obligation can be expensive, of course, but more importantly, it is *time-consuming*. At the outset of our story, Gabriel has recently come to understand what this means for him. Even without the responsibilities of a landlord, the time investment that Gabriel's work demands from him already puts him at risk of becoming like the absent father depicted in Harry Chapin's classic song, "The Cat's in the Cradle." Had he decided to invest in single-family homes, that situation would have worsened, eating up whatever free time he had left—and depriving him of the only opportunity he would ever have to be a good father to Tony.

We are all put on this Earth for a finite number of hours. With that in mind, imagine having to deal with some tenant's broken water heater or a burst pipe at two o'clock in the morning.

Time, not money, is the most precious resource we have. In Gabriel's case, the passive income provided by his investments in apartment syndications preserved his valuable free time while still allowing him to maintain the lifestyle he and Tony enjoyed. That passive income kept him from becoming entangled in the day-today "toilets and tenants" nuisances of being a landlord, thereby enabling him to pursue a relationship with Elena.

Time is the first and most important difference between investing in multifamily apartments and investing in single-family homes—but of course, it is not the *only* important consideration. While it is (in our opinion) less important than time, money is hardly a trivial concern.

Elena certainly was very concerned about money. Although she was successful, she was not independently wealthy—unlike Gabriel. That is why she was perpetually waffling, forever on the fence about committing to an investment. It had taken her years to earn that money and years to acquire the education that made it possible for her to earn it. She was not a gambler by nature; indeed, her innate risk aversion made the stock market unattractive to her.

Elena doesn't like surprises—a personality trait that extends to her preference for vanilla ice cream (when she indulges in sweets). That trait would have made single-family homes a disastrous investment for her for a number of reasons.

First, unexpected repair costs are incredibly common in single-family homes. Unless you are an experienced, *full-time* investor, you simply don't have time for the kind of due diligence and legwork required to minimize those kinds of surprises.

When you purchase a single-family home on your own, you don't know what kinds of hidden headaches may have slipped past whoever performed the inspection. That's not necessarily because the seller intentionally deceived you (although they may have). It's simply impossible to know what unsuspected problems may be lurking in the plumbing, the wiring, the foundation, or who knows where else.

And then, of course, there are the tenants, whom you must find, evaluate, and vet—and who also can surprise us in unpleasant ways. If they don't pay their rent, you can be stuck with them until you're able to evict them—which is easier in some states than in others. And lawyers are expensive.

Even after you finally manage to evict a deadbeat tenant—which can take several months—you're back at square one. You'll still have to paint, and you'll need to inspect the place for any damage they may have done. And if the house remains vacant for a long time, you've got no money coming in and *a lot* of money going out.

At the root, all these potential problems can be traced back to the fact that a single-family home is an *active* investment, no different from a taco truck or a dental practice.

An apartment syndication, on the other hand, is a *passive* investment. Your only commitment is financial; everything else is taken care of for you. *We* inspect the property. *We* handle any renovations that need to be done, and *we* find tenants to occupy the units. We also collect the rent and handle any issues the tenants may have. And if a tenant needs to be evicted for any reason, it's our in-house management team, not you, who will have to have that uncomfortable conversation.

Why REEP Is Different

Of course, we know we're not the only operators in this field. So why should you invest with us rather than another organization?

The biggest differentiator is the in-house management that we provide. Most other apartment syndicators use third-party management companies. After they close on a property, they hand it over to another company that brings in *their* team, *their* approach to the management of the property, and (often) *their* approach to the renovation process. Maybe their values align with the investors' values . . . and maybe they don't. Either way, the day-to-day management of your investment is one step further removed from you than it otherwise would have been and, therefore, more opaque to you. And, of course, that extra layer of bureaucracy increases costs for the whole enterprise.

By way of contrast, a dollar invested with *REEP* stays with REEP because we have our own management company. As soon as we accept your money and close on the property, we manage that money all the way to disposition. We have control over who we hire. Just as important, we have control over the policies we implement to keep the team happy. And if the team is happy, the residents are happy because they know the team is going to take care of them.

And so, it's important to us that our vision for that property is shared from day one through closing. It's ingrained in our team, and the minute we close, they hit the ground running to make whatever upgrades to the property are necessary to make it a better community, to open our arms with a duty of care to the tenants, to drive up rents and all the other factors that make a property more valuable.

You never take better care of anything than what belongs to you.

The other important differentiator is experience and a successful track record as a visionary and entrepreneur. Jacob started his first company at the age of twenty-six. That company was Property Automation Software, the number-one selling property management software program for property management companies. PAS had 21,000 customers in nine countries and managed more than 3.9 million units. He grew organically with no venture capital and no debt. Jacob sold it as the sole shareholder in 2007, and we moved to San Antonio. That's when we bought our first twenty-four-unit apartment complex.

Arleen has a degree in Business Administration in Finance and is a former Bank of America executive. She was in banking for twenty years and served in various key roles in the financial services industry, achieving the title of Senior Vice President. She also served as National Hispanic Marketing Manager, Retail Banking Center Manager, International Private Banking Manager and as a Credit Officer. While in these roles, Arleen appeared on national and local media programs providing personal financial management education to consumers in Spanish and English.

Finally, we are both certified apartment managers and certified apartment portfolio supervisors through the National Apartment Association.

We Would Love to Hear From You!

If you have money that you want to invest in something that will return handsomely with little risk, you should consider investing in real estate. If you value your time and mental health more than anything else, consider investing in multifamily apartment buildings rather than single-family homes.

If you want to invest in multifamily apartment buildings with the guidance of an experienced team that values transparency and conducts business conscientiously and ethically, then we should talk.

To learn more about us, visit https://reepequity.com/ and send us a message or just e-mail us at Invest@reepequity.com.

We don't have to consider it a date . . . but it may be the start of a valuable relationship.

About the Authors

The Garzas, founders of REEP (Real Estate Equity Partners) in 2012, have built a powerful partnership that drives the company's success with a focus on both financial returns and social impact. They believe in the principles of impact investing, where investors can meet their financial goals while contributing to the development of great communities where families can live and thrive.

Together, they lead REEP's strategic vision and growth, overseeing more than $730 million in acquisitions across 6,700 units. By identifying underperforming multifamily properties and implementing value-add improvements, the Garzas have consistently optimized investor returns while prioritizing community well-being.

The Garzas understand that apartment investing can significantly contribute to building family legacy wealth. Multifamily properties offer steady cash flow and long-term appreciation, making them an ideal tool for creating generational wealth. Through REEP, the Garzas help families use real estate as a key part of their wealth-building strategies, ensuring financial security for future generations

The Garza Foundation's donation to the Thru Project,
a cause that helps young adults who age out of the foster care system

The Garza's speaking. Reach out to have them speak at your event

A REEP Residential team member in the Texas 100-degree heat wearing a REEP provided cooling vest and shade umbrella

All Texas team members at the annual strategic retreat

REEP Investors gather on buses to tour their properties

The REEP Team – Award winners for being one of the 25 fastest growing companies in San Antonio. REEP is a 6-time winner.

The Garza family, Jacob, Arleen, Victoria and Jack